Poetry In Motion
The Awakening

By Bryan Brumley
My Name Is Nobody

Copyright © 2023
All rights reserved.

No part of this book may be reproduced or
transmitted in any form or by any means, electronic or mechanical,
including photocopying, recording, or by any information storage
and retrieval system, without permission in writing from the
copyright owner.

Published by
GRAPH Publishing, L.L.C.
www.graphpublishing.com

Printed in the U.S.A.

Dedication

First and foremost, I would like to give credit and thank to our Heavenly Father, Jesus Christ our Lord and Savior, and the Holy Ghost. I thank my Heavenly Father for loving and caring enough to take even a millisecond to help and save such a selfish creation. I thank the Father for having the patience to see his plan of salvation through. For giving us all a chance to not only accept it, but to share it also. I thank Jesus for his sacrifice. For having enough love to do it for all that would merely believe in him and what he both said and did. I thank him for living the example that is meant to help keep us on the straight and narrow path. I thank the Holy Ghost for his guidance and comfort. For inspiring all that believe and for testifying to truth for all that truly ask, seek then knock.

While I dedicate this book to the ones that inspired it, I thank my help mate, my wife and partner in this spiritual battlefield here on Earth. I thank her for sticking with me through not just the bad parts of our lives and marriage, but through my initial shaping and molding process. She patiently listened to my babbling as this book came together over the years. I also thank the readers. I pray that the Holy Ghost moves in the lives of everyone, even those that would throw stones and harsh judgments. I pray that this movement of the Holy Ghost leads many to believe and trust in Jesus Christ as their Lord, Savior and example. Amen.

Playlist

I Pledge Allegiance To The Lamb - Ray Boltz

I Want To Be Just Like You - Phillips Craig and Dean

In The House - Crowder

Son Of David - Ryan Ellis

Don't Tread On Me - We the Kingdom

Back To The Garden - Crowder

Crushing Snakes - Crowder

Don't Understand - Rare of breed

Let It Go - Bryann Trejo

This I Pray - Nicky Gracious

Living Water - Bryann Trejo

Christian Muzic - Kingdom muzic

Privilege - Young bro

Stand Up - Nicky Gracious

Jesus Called My Name - Zauntee

Loving On My Enemies - Bryann Trejo

Background - Lecrae

Godtwang - Rare of breed

Galgotha Hill - Crowder

Red Letters - Crowder

Watch The Lamb - Ray Boltz

Introduction

Contrary to appearances, my purpose is not to go around beating people in the head with a bible. My only purpose is to share how Jesus still works in our lives today through the Holy Ghost. That when we learn to slow our lives back down to one day at a time and take Jesus seriously, we can better see the poetry in motion that is the Lord working hard to work all things out for good through the Holy Ghost. Even the plans of lucifer that are meant for evil will be turned to good, just as the very death of Jesus was meant for evil but God the Father used it for the greatest good.

This book is also a story of a piece that Jesus commissioned me to do as well as important biblical lessons for our times. This piece works as a visual aid only, for biblical lessons, and as a reminder of why Moses had to raise a brass serpent on a pole in Numbers 21:5-9. After reading that story, it is no wonder why Jesus himself makes mention of it in John 3:14,15.

John 3:14,15

14) "And as Moses lifted up the serpent in the wilderness, even so must the son of man be
lifted up:
15) That whosoever believeth in him should not perish, but have eternal life".

If there ever was a time to remember a story of what a people had to do to fix a problem, it is now. The fault is in our increased selfishness and forgetting where our blessings come from. The cure is to turn our eyes back on Jesus and his words, examples and the most important, his sacrifice on the cross and what it means for us all. Just as God's people needed a visual aid to remind them of God the Father and to test their obedience, we need one in these days to remind us of Jesus and what price he paid for our selfishness, which God the Father again uses as a test of our ability to believe and obey. It is forgetting these things that gets us into trouble. This is why he himself references to the brass serpent, which foreshadows what Jesus was to do and be for us all.

There is a story behind the commissioning of this piece, which is too long to bring into this introduction. Aside from the biblical lessons this piece helps with, which I speak of in this book, this piece helps with making sure that no matter who I am talking to about our Lord and Savior Jesus Christ, they know I am talking about the only one who ever died on the cross for the selfishness of humanity. My intentions are not to offend anyone by using the name Jesus either. We sometimes become so single minded that we forget that he is known by many names but by only one spirit, the Holy Ghost, which is the one thing lucifer cannot copy. So when I talk of the lessons of our Lord and Savior, they are the lessons of Jesus Christ, the only one who sacrificed himself on a cross to finish for all that would believe, the law of sacrifice.

In this book, I share my experience that brought me to the making of this piece, not to draw attention to myself. I have already been guilty of reaching for too much already. I only share it to show that Jesus is still working in each of our lives through the Holy Ghost in these days as well. To show that Jesus is waiting for each of us to reach a certain realization so he can move mountains through us. I do my best to explain questions that hold many back from the walk with Jesus that helps us to heal. I share a few experiences that my wife and I have had while traveling over three hundred thousand miles all across the United States with this commissioned piece, trying to share who we need to turn our eyes back to as a nation to fix what our selfishness has broken. Not to lift my selfish ego, but to show the poetry in motion of Jesus working through the Holy Ghost through each of us, as we learn to slow back down to one day at a time.

I also cover lessons that many have trouble speaking of

and some that we have forgotten and were told to remember. I do not speak of anything new, for there is nothing new under the sun. Only things our selfishness has allowed us to forget and allowed lucifer and his system of thought to infiltrate too deeply and hide, all to stop us from being ready for Jesus's second coming. I explain truths that many will see as attacks because as the Apostle Paul explains how people will be in certain times in 2 Timothy 4:3,4, people will ignore sound doctrine and turn a blind eye and deaf ear to biblical truths to continue living a lie. The only thing I point out is the system of thought of lucifer's. The very system of thought that Jesus points out that infiltrated the minds of the religious leaders of Jesus's day. The very system of thought that is alive and well today trying to do the same things to Christ's church, his bride.

    The only purpose of this piece and book is to remind any that may have forgotten from time to time, including myself, of why we need to remember to keep our eyes on the cross and what took place there. Of what it means for humanity and each of us as individuals. To remind us that we are here for a reason and that there is an enemy that is bent on stopping humanity from returning home to the Father, because misery loves company. I pray that the Holy Ghost will move in the lives of all that read and that he will open our eyes and ears to the truths we allowed lucifer to keep hidden. I pray blessings on all as we walk day by day with Jesus and seek the kingdom of God and what it is like over anything else.

Love Lots & Pray Often
One Day At A Time
My Name Is Nobody

Table Of Contents

The Virus And The Vaccine	13
Why Jesus	19
Why Pray	35
When Jesus Calls Our Name	43
One Day At A Time	49
The Case For The Seventh Day	57
For The Profit Of All	81
Seeds By The Wayside	107
The Great Commission	137
To See A Revival	143
Poetry In Motion	159
Author's Note	169
About the Author	173

THE VIRUS AND THE VACCINE

Now I am not sure if everyone has heard of the virus outbreak that happened a very long time ago. This virus has wiped out entire cities and almost wiped out humanity at least once. In those days, we did not have the vaccine for this virus, only the treatments. So it was a huge blessing when the vaccine was finally delivered. Unfortunately, the carrier of the vaccine was murdered by his own people, because there is more money and control in treatments than in cures, sound familiar? The bad news is that this virus is still around today threatening to destroy families, friends, governments, cultures and even religion; and for the same reasons. Authorities do not take this virus and vaccine seriously and too many people simply do not know about the vaccine, or just will not take it. Much of this is due to a world that is busy trying to hide the fact that this virus and vaccine even exists.

The virus is called selfishness and was transferred to humanity by patient "zero", Aka. lucifer. The virus is born into each person and the symptoms of this virus are highly contagious and is spread by a teaching method called monkey see, monkey do. This method of transfer is one of the ways the symptoms become hereditary, passing from one generation to another. Symptoms of this highly contagious virus will be one or more of the following; thoughts or feelings of Envy, Gluttony, Greed, Lust, Pride, Sloth or Wrath. Each of these individual ailments produce their own side effects but all are a direct result of the virus of selfishness. The killers of the vaccine carrier were eaten up with many of these symptoms due to lucifer, ever so slowly working his system of thought into the religious leaders of the day. Therefore their eyes and their hearts were not able to see the vaccine for who and what he was. The symptoms along with their severity will vary from person to person. Since we already know that we all are infected by this virus, the test given is more to measure our level of infection.

Luke 7:47

47) "Wherefore I say to you, her sins, which are many, are forgiven, for she loved much. But to whom little is forgiven, the same loves little."

Matthew 7:16

16) "Ye shall know them by their fruits."

These two scriptures teach us to watch how we treat others, for it tells a message to others on where we stand with the Father. Wealth does not show our faith because one does not need God to obtain it. The repetition of history shows us this lesson plainly. How we treat others does however show our faith, or lack of. If we have the vaccine and are forgiven much, we love lots and resist selfishness with love, kindness and forgiveness. If we do not have the vaccine, we randomly become engulfed in one or more symptoms and our actions show it. Simply put, we will know the highly infected by the way they treat others. Not just how they treat their friends and family either. But also how they treat their enemies and those that do them wrong. This last is the true test of our character. When someone does us wrong, are we quick to dish out rage and the harshest punishments from the heart of lucifer? Or do we try to react first with love, understanding and the heart of Jesus?

Luke 6:32

32) "For if you love them which love you, what good are you? For even the wicked do the same."

The good news about the vaccine is that in lucifer's attempt to destroy, hide and/or change the vaccine, he released it making it available for anyone, anywhere at any time. We only have to ask with a sincere heart. The vaccine is free as it should be if our goal is truly for the profit of all humanity. The vaccine is unlimited and only has to be taken once. The bad news is that there is an undisclosed time limit to get the vaccine. The vaccine is required to leave quarantine and go home to the Father that is waiting for his prideful and prodigal children to make the journey home. All before he turns up the furnace to eradicate the virus completely. The other bit of news is that there is only one vaccine.

John 14:6

6) Jesus said unto him, "I am the way, the truth and the life: No man cometh to the father, but by me."

The vaccine is a two part shot consisting of both faith and works and unfortunately only works together. Many plagued by slothfulness ignore works thinking they can be saved by what is reserved for those that die shortly after receiving Jesus as lord and savior, as in the case of the thief on the cross possibly, because the scriptures do not say that the thief had never been baptized. Our refusal to work as the great commission commands, has some of us forget that our faith is only seen by others through our works. Hence we will know them by their fruits. If not for the works that show our faith, the scriptures would not be, because the laziness caused by selfishness would have all of the world believe that works are not needed. How far would the plan of salvation go if nobody believed in works?

James 2:17

17) Even so faith, if it has not works, is dead, being alone.

I find myself pretending that We are falling, which we all are, and Jesus is going to reach out and catch us. Now our works is the measure of our reach to Jesus. So we have to give him something to grab onto, even if it is only a "T" rex arm. Our faith is the measure of Jesus's reach to us. You know in the movies where someone is falling and we just know that they fell past the point of reaching? Then bam! Somehow the other person reaches out with a go-go gadget arm. Our faith turns

Jesus's arm into a go-go gadget arm. Some might say that this is putting a limitation on Jesus. Some will always argue to avoid work. This is not a limitation placed by man but a requirement and law put in place by God the Father. If we are not willing to give Jesus the tiniest thing to grab, do we deserve heaven?

    Once taken, the vaccine will force an inward look in a mirror which is why I believe so many refuse the vaccine. It is even why the world itself is preparing, by teaching not to look at what and who is coming and to laugh at any idea for the profit of all. We know that Jesus will awaken us through the Holy Ghost, yet the world has even turned the term of being awakened as being bad, just as the world twisted the true meaning of the rainbow. Once we do look, we begin to see things under a different light, the light of Christ. We begin to understand how the virus works and the importance of the vaccine and taking the daily boosters which are loving and forgiving each other. Kindness is like vitamin C boosting our spiritual immune system. Love, kindness and forgiveness are repellents to the symptoms of the virus and the highly infected are repelled by the vaccine. If one does not believe this, randomly start talking about Jesus and the truths in the Bible and see if the highly infected do not walk away, get argumentative or even violent.

John 15:18,21,23

18)   "If the world hate you, Ye know that it hated me before it hated you."
21)   "But all these things will they do unto you for my name's sake, because they know not him that sent me."
23)   "He that hateth me hateth my father also."

    After the inward look and we dry our eyes and maybe even get up off of the floor, we feel a renewed strength and purpose. A purpose to tell the world about this virus that lucifer has tried to keep hidden and about the vaccine that he tried to destroy. My goal is to travel the U.S. with the project that the Holy Ghost commissioned me to do, to use as a visual aid only, in advertising the Jesus vaccine. For those that wish me well, thank you and God bless. To those that do not wish me well, God bless anyway and remember, there is a time limit on taking the Jesus vaccination and that time limit is different for each person and as we are taught, one hundred percent of the population must receive the Jesus vaccine to save one hundred percent of the population.

WHY JESUS

If I was asked this question only three years before writing this, I would only say what I have heard so many others say without really knowing what it meant. At age forty-six, I have been baptized into two different body parts or denominations and have done a lot of bible reading, yet for me, it took what I call an Apostle Paul moment to finally start understanding the answer to this question. I call it my Apostle Paul moment because even though I have always believed in our Heavenly Father, I have not always fully believed in Jesus and the bible. That is why I will be found saying now that Jesus has always been with me, even though I have not always been with him. A part of me would always try to say, "many of us might have been able to go through what he did if we had the support and witness of angels like he did". Or, "I can't trust a book written by man's hand." That is where we see envy rearing its ugly head. At times, I tried to be like someone I was not even sure was real. The world does a good job at creating so many false things to believe in and celebrate, it is no wonder our youth have trouble believing in the story of Jesus. One could say at times I believed in Jesus, only not enough to believe Jesus and to take his words seriously, there is a difference. I wanted to believe but I had trust issues, many of which were caused by the world's desire to make up false things to believe in.

What helped me to relate to the Apostle Paul was that he believed in Jesus also but did not believe Jesus's words. Paul knew Jesus had lived and died on a cross. He hunted and persecuted the believers of Jesus because he did not believe the words Jesus spoke, just like so many these days. Until he had an experience that opened his eyes and heart to Jesus and his mission. While I did not persecute believers, I did however speak words to my child that I have to work the rest of my life to fix. As my selfish and unbalanced life led me deeper into alcoholism, I drunkenly told my son one night that I did not believe Jesus was real. In my opinion, this was the straw that broke the camel's back for Jesus.

    A good bit of my problem began when I started chasing oilfield money and letting my job become my identity. I spent about fourteen years climbing the ladder of "success". I worked seven days a week and worked eight to sixteen hours each day. I worked the first three years with no vacation, always cashing it in to keep working. I was finding out how not remembering the Sabbath day of rest could wear his children down. On that journey, I noticed a common thing in all of the supervisors I worked for and had seen. They were all over worked, underpaid and used alcohol to cope with the constant stress of being asked to do more and more, faster and faster, with no more than a pat on the back and a "that a boy". I noticed it enough that when I was asked to move up to tool pusher, a supervisor's position, I turned it down twice. When the company owner asked me why, I shared my concerns with him. After being convinced that those things would not happen to me, I took the job. I honestly felt like he might help me to not get into that situation. Fast forward about five years and I was drinking from the time I woke up to the time I went to bed, and telling my son one day that Jesus is not real. I'm guessing the owner simply did not believe that the job itself created that kind of stress. I do want to make known that I do not tell this story to pass off blame or to receive pity. The blame for our own actions will always lay with us, and this story is a tale of lessons learned and battles won. I would not even mention myself but in order to give Jesus credit, I have to tell the story of his poetry in motion in not just my life, but in each of our lives. If we did not share what Jesus has done or is doing in our lives, again, we would not have the scriptures. Jesus did not say he only worked in the apostles' lives and would work in none others. Sharing what Jesus does in our lives is how we encourage each other from generation to generation, because it shows that Jesus is still moving today in our times.

    I am thankful for Jesus's mercy because he could have let me continue until a tragedy happened, because I was doing a lot of drinking and driving. Instead, he inspired me to change jobs as the oilfield continued its cycle of a downward slope. I was at the point that my wife did not know what to do anymore, and my children saw a dad they did not want to be like anymore. That last one is what really got me. Most of our child's lives I would sing to them my favorite song by Phillips Craig and Dean called "*I want to be just like you.*" It has always been kind of my compass. I became so busy chasing other stuff that I never realized that I had lost my way because I couldn't find it in me to sing the song to myself. My wife could not even talk to me about my drinking because I would always say that I had it under control. She would try to talk to me when I was sober but I started drinking most times before she even got up. Luckily some friends introduced me to delivering camper trailers across the United States. I had to pretty much quit drinking because I had to follow the same DOT rules as semi drivers. Even though I was still driving hard because of the debt I acquired making oilfield money, it was still fairly stress free.

    Things were going pretty good until I checked on a good friend one day. I had gotten a message back from his phone, which was from his cousin in Georgia. It said that he was sorry to let me know that he died a few days after a motorcycle accident involving drinking and riding. One would think that this would keep a person sober. We all come up with excuses to justify the reasons for our actions. I let this loss that I was never taught how to deal with push me back into drinking. The biggest problem was now I was drinking and driving across the United States. I did not know how to cope with the loss and spent the first forty-eight hours driving and drinking because I could not close my eyes without breaking down. I couldn't even go into a restaurant so I didn't eat, only drank. I started drinking and driving until I stopped at night and passed out, just to do it again the next day. It was only by the grace of God that I did not hurt or kill myself or someone else during all of this. My wife caught on and we decided she was going to hire on and drive along with me, because being alone all of the time made things worse and being trapped by my own debt kept me on the road.

I was coming across I80 to meet my wife in Indiana for her orientation. Only I did not show up the night I was supposed to. I had drank so much that I passed out while driving and drove about two hundred miles, in the wrong direction I believe. I woke up parked at a gas station with my needle on empty and my auxiliary hose sticking out of my tank, which meant I stopped somewhere to try to put fuel in. I was missing a flip flop and had vomit all over my shirt. I had no memory of how I had gotten where I was, a literal Jesus take the wheel moment.

When everything really sank in, I felt a familiar presence next to me that I remembered as a child. It was the warm, compassionate, peaceful and loving feeling that comes with a sense that everything will be alright. This feeling only comes from the Holy Ghost because these are the things that define him, and the one thing that lucifer cannot copy because these things are not in him. While I did not hear a voice or anything, I felt him tell me or impress on me that if I did not do what I was supposed to, he could not protect me from my ignorance anymore. At that moment, I knew if I did this again, I would either end up killing myself, someone else or both. I had a realization of what abusing God's grace meant and I had been abusing it greatly. This is also one of those times where those under lucifer's system of thought would argue that God does not make threats to accomplish his will. I would have to say to quit being so eager to argue that one misreads what is said. I was not threatened, I was merely told that I will not be protected if I chose to continue the path I was choosing for myself, that simple, nothing more nothing less. I apologized to Jesus and asked him to help me. This was the moment that I realized I cannot do everything on my own and was never expected to. Even though I had been baptized twice, like so many, I was not truly where I was supposed to be spiritually until this experience, until this understanding that the Holy Ghost is waiting for each of us to reach. My glass was finally empty waiting to be filled by the Holy Ghost, so I thought. Jesus is waiting for each person to come to this realization so the real walk with him can begin. The Holy Ghost inspired me to go through a forty day fast. I became aware of the words of Jesus to his apostles, who could not heal the son of a particular man that approaches Jesus for help.

Mark 9:29

29)   And he said unto them,"This kind can come forth by nothing, but by prayer and fasting."

Jesus told his apostles that fasting and prayer is required to get rid of certain unclean spirits. Jesus had not made the apostles fast yet because as he told the Pharisees when they asked, the bridegroom is still with them.

Mark 2:19

19)   And Jesus said unto them, "can the children of the bridegroom fast, while the bridegroom is with them? As long as they have the bridegroom with them, they cannot fast."

I would like to note that not everyone has to have an Apostle Paul moment to reach this understanding and not everyone is called to do a forty day fast, my stubbornness was just that strong. So I started a forty day fast in January of 2020. I ate nothing but peanut butter and honey for forty days. I drank no coffee or sugary drinks and I only listened to christian music. I did not watch T.V. programming, only drove, read the bible or listened to christian programs and slept for forty days. I did not listen to any particular christian station alone because when driving across the country, stations come and go about every sixty miles or so. They are all a single part of a body anyway. I did all of this not to break chains that Jesus's sacrifice already unlocked, but for the strength to put down those chains and quit picking them back up. Many of us are running around being weighed down by unlocked chains. I'm sure it hurts Jesus to watch us trying to break what he unlocked with his sacrifice. The examples of Jesus show us how to put them down and leave them there. It is our selfishness and our decisions daily to not take Jesus's words and examples seriously that have us keep picking up old chains. Then when we feel we cannot do it on our own because of our unbelief, We pick lucifer's system of thought back up and browbeat the world to accept those faults we won't let go of. All so we can feel better about our selfish ways.

    I thought that this was the beginning of what I was inspired to call his poetry in motion. Turns out I was already in the middle of this story of the Holy Ghost working in all of our lives, like an app working in the background that we do not notice, until we slow our lives down enough to honestly look. It was during this forty day fast that the lord not only showed me how to put down chains of addiction through fasting and prayer, but that he is real and can be believed and taken seriously. As I turned myself to him completely, he not only started a change in me, he commissioned me to use the talents and material possessions he blesses me with to tell of him. To remind everyone of who we need to put our eyes back on, to cure us all of the selfish venom that lucifer has injected us all with. We are all born into original sin which is selfishness. Each one of us is guilty of selfishness and the law and Jesus points this out.

    So what would I say today to the question of why Jesus? After three years so far of trying to live one day at a time, I would say that it is because he is our rock, anchor and our foundation. Even after losing a dad and a best friend. No loss of a loved one is greater than another. A loss is a loss and the pain and sometimes regrets felt is real in any and all losses. Only now do I understand. Jesus tells us that this world and everything in it is temporary. Everything will rust, rot, age and turn to dust or ash one day. I know that we do not like to admit it, but the moment anything is born in this world, it starts dying. This is why he tells us not to love anything or anyone more than him. That if we love something or someone more than him, we do not deserve him. This does not mean that we cannot weep and grieve over a loss. Jesus's own example with

Lazarus shows that grieving is ok, but our true belief in Jesus and his promises do not let us stay there for too long. Which becomes another way for us to measure our level of belief in not only Jesus himself, but in his words also. This is what makes Jesus our rock, anchor and foundation. Everything and everyone else we build a house on will sink us.

John 14:6,7

6)   Jesus saith unto him, "I am the way, the truth, and the life: No man cometh unto the father, but by me.
7)   If ye had known me, ye should have known my father also: And from henceforth ye know him, and seen him."

Jesus was sent to us for multiple reasons. This is why I say that Jesus is a master of killing multiple birds with one stone, or teaching multiple lessons with one parable. Jesus, through his life, became the perfect example for all of humanity to follow. How he lived his life, how he treated people and interacted with them is the way we are supposed to be. We can model and imitate anyone that we want, but modeling Jesus is the only way that will help us through our selfishness. Not in a way that makes everyone the same like robots. We are each different with unique gifts and talents. We are to become alike in heart and mind with a desire that everything is done for the profit of all not self alone. Just as a husband and wife become one, not as one person but as one heart and spirit with the family in mind as a whole, not individuals only. It is in this way that when a husband and wife have been together in a healthy marriage for a long time, when we meet only one of them, we have met the other also in nature because the two have the same nature. They will be of the same mind.

The ten commandments point out what sin is for us and what we need to stay away from. We were then given sacrifices in order to pay for a particular sin that we could not stay away from. This was known as the law of sacrifice. Jesus came along and showed us that the root of every sin that humanity commits comes from original sin called selfishness. We can analyze any problem in the world from an argument between friends to world hunger, war and even child trafficking. When boiled all of the way down, selfishness is at the core. Selfishness is why lucifer did what he did, in heaven and in the garden. Selfishness is why Eve was so easily fooled by lucifer. Selfishness is why Cain killed Abel. We can look at any bad deed ever done and see selfishness as the mother of whatever sin was committed, making selfishness original sin. Before Jesus came along, All we could do was treat the symptoms of selfishness, by performing sacrifices to admit our sin and as a way of telling God that we were sorry. The selfishness of greed infected the Scribes and the Pharisees as they realized how much money was going to be made selling to the people for sacrifices. Lucifer had injected them with his selfish venom and is why Jesus called them out regularly.

John 8:38,44
38) "I speak that which I have seen with my father: And you do that which ye have seen with your father.
44) Ye are of your father the devil, and the lusts of your father ye will do."

Their greed saw people's never ending sins as a way to get rich, and since sacrifices were a law of God, until the Messiah came, they became the dealer for forgiveness, thinking that they could control and sell salvation. This way of thinking and being is what Jesus said they were doing from their father the devil. They became infected by lucifer's system of thought. The severity of our sin determined our sacrifice. Some even believed that the more expensive the sacrifice or the more money was gifted, the more one was forgiven. Sound familiar? Nothing new under the sun. Many that traveled long distances for temple work had to buy their sacrifice in the city, which eventually became available at the temple itself, which opened up the need to have money changers at the temple. One can almost see the Pharisees wringing their greedy hands like a raccoon, then enters Jesus.

Matthew 21:12,13

12) And Jesus went into the temple of God, and cast out all them that sold and bought in the temple. And overthrew the tables of the moneychangers, and the seats of them that sold doves,

13) And said unto them, "It is written, my house shall be called the house of prayer, but ye have made it a den of thieves."

This was one of the few times that Jesus showed anger, letting us know that there are some things worth getting angry about. Also that he is not pleased when a place that is supposed to be a house of prayer, becomes more concerned about money than the needs of those coming to pray. This is where we should remember the lesson from Judas. That even one that followed Jesus, ate with him and learned from him, can be corrupted by the love of money, and it corrupts our interpretations and perceptions. Each sin would have us twist different scriptures only to justify why wewill not let go of a particular sin. In this case it was the Pharisees' sin of control and greed. Jesus saw salvation and forgiveness being dammed up and parceled out making the flock go thirsty, all for selfish reasons. Jesus's suffering and sacrifice on the cross was where he became the life. This is why he said as he was dying that "it is finished".

John 19:30

30) When Jesus therefore had received the vinegar, he said, "It is finished": And he bowed his head, and gave up the ghost.

This is also what Jesus was talking about when he said that he came not to change the law, but to fulfill it. Jesus was making it clear that he did not come to change any of the laws previously given. We are still selfish in need of a sacrifice to pay for our selfishness against God the Father. Jesus only simplified the commandments/law, he did not change a one, nor did he change or do away with any sabbaths. Jesus did not change the law of sacrifice, he fulfilled it with his sacrifice.

Matthew 5:17,18

17) "Think not that I am come to destroy the law, or the prophets: I am not come to destroy, but to fulfill.
18) For verily I say unto you, till heaven and earth pass, one jot or one tittle shall in no wise pass from the law, till all be fulfilled."

It amazes me how often Jesus speaks plainly about not doing something or calling ourselves something, then we turn right around and do it and even build a religion around some disobediences. His purpose through his sacrifice was to fulfill the law of sacrifice. All sacrifices, even verbal ones. The law of equivalent exchange says that something can only be bought and paid for by giving something of equal value. We could sacrifice every living thing on earth and never come close to paying for our selfishness against God the Father. Jesus became that sacrifice and anyone saying that we have to do more belittles his sacrifice, saying that it was not good enough. Simple as that. Sacrifices were a way of telling God that we recognize our sin and that we were sorry. Just like baptisms today, some did it with true intent and some did it for show, only God truly knows.Now all that is needed for forgiveness is to believe in Jesus and what he did. Jesus became our high priest, we no longer need a human to tell us that we have to sacrifice this to be forgiven, or we have to say so many of those or pay so much money. We now start the redemption process by repenting of our selfishness and becoming baptized. Now that lucifer knows that all is required is belief, repentance and baptism for forgiveness, do we think he left well enough alone after Jesus's death? Do we really think he did not continue to use his system of thought to make selfish men find a way to control things like baptisms now? We have to continually remind ourselves of Jesus's words and actions so we can recognize when someone is following in the mistakes of the Scribes and Pharisees, trying to control forgiveness and salvation.

We need to remember that believing in Jesus also means believing Jesus. We can believe someone existed and not believe in their words and actions. If we believe in and on Jesus, we listen to his words and take him seriously. We do not listen to the same line lucifer used in the garden,

Genesis 3:4
4) And the serpent said unto the woman, ye shall not surely die.

Lucifer from the beginning of creation has tried to call God the Father a liar, all to convince us that he is not serious about the words that he says and the commandments that he gives. Again, God is always shining light on lucifer's system of thought by saying not to do something. Knowing that lucifer cannot help but to twist God's words to trick mankind into doing what was commanded not to do. When we allow lucifer to trick us into thinking that Jesus was not serious about our salvation, he becomes the bird plucking away the seed that is the word of God dropped by the wayside.

Matthew 13:3,4
3) And he spake many things unto them in parables, saying, "Behold, a sower went forth to sow;
4) And when he sowed, some seeds fell by the wayside, and the fowls came and devoured them up"

Matthew 13:19
19) "When any one heareth the word of the kingdom, and understandeth it not, then cometh the wicked one, and catcheth away that which was sown in his heart. This is he which received seed by the wayside."

When we do not understand and start to ask questions, lucifer robs this seed trying to sprout by trying to discredit the words of Jesus by saying, "oh, he wasn't serious when he said that". Sounds an awful lot like the serpent in the garden. Lucifer also makes many feel bad for even having any questions. Jesus tells us that we are to ask, seek and knock.

Matthew 7:7,8

7) "Ask, and it shall be given you; seek, and ye shall find; Knock, and it shall be opened unto you:

8) For every one that asketh receiveth; and he that seeketh findeth; and to him that knocketh it shall be opened."

We are supposed to want to learn and to learn starts with asking questions. When we start asking, this begins the desire to seek. Then we start knocking and the Holy Ghost opens the doors of our understanding. It starts with asking and the enemy is good about stopping us from looking by telling us that "He was not serious when he said that". When we believe this lie, we tend to never get to the seeking part, which leads to never knocking, which leads to our understanding never being opened. We continue to depend on someone other than Jesus for our forgiveness and when we do not think we can afford their price, we give up, slipping back into our selfishness which continues to produce the sins that plague humanity. These are the reasons for the question of why Jesus. He is the way because his life was the perfect example for us to follow, not just to overcome our own selfishness, but to be able to return home to the Father also. He is the truth because he opens our eyes to our own selfishness and introduces us to the nature and purpose of God the Father through his own words and actions.

John 14:7

7) "If ye had known me, ye should have known my father also: And from henceforth ye know him, and have seen him."

Jesus teaches and shows us to overcome selfishness with selflessness. To put it in a way that many youth might understand, Jesus teaches and shows the truth of lucifer's system of thought being one of all for one, which leads to chaos and destruction on a road paved with greed, hate and division. At the same time, Jesus shows his system of thought of one for all that leads to love, life and time everlasting on a road paved with forgiveness and selfless acts. Jesus was showing us what heaven on earth would look like, if we would only think of what would profit all in all of our thoughts and actions. Jesus is the life because of his death and resurrection. His resurrection is the proof to us of his promises to us, that there is life after death with him in heaven. If Jesus did not rise, then he did not prove he can defeat death for us all. Belief in his resurrection is why we do not mourn for long, because we truly believe that we will see them again with Jesus, as long as we were taught these lessons instead of the lessons of the world, as long as we were taught to believe instead of to laugh and mock. Believing in the resurrections of both Lazarus and Jesus should give us strength in the promises of Jesus. Because of the sacrifice of Jesus, the price for the selfishness of all humanity was paid. The law of equivalent exchange was upheld with the voluntary death of an innocent lamb and the law of sacrifice fulfilled and finished on the cross, creating a way home for both the prodigal and prideful children that would merely believe and obey. Jesus unlocked the chains of selfishness that were going to make us the property of lucifer. All we have to do now is believe in what he did for us, and set those unlocked chains down and walk that straight and narrow path which is his example that he set for all. We then become baptized into the body of Christ where the Holy Ghost continues to shape, mold, guide and direct us on our work to help in this mission to share the news of Jesus and what he did for all, and to strengthen us for the change that occurs on this walk with Jesus. We often go off on side trails thinking we can get to God on a shortcut. We always end up lost. Only when we learn to calm down and put our eyes back on Jesus, do we find our way back to the right path. Only to find we are back on the path we thought we could shortcut, because there is only one way and that is Jesus and his examples and sacrifice.

    I pray that this helps anyone that struggles with the question of why Jesus. I pray that we all will continue to ask, seek and knock. I pray that we will take the life of Jesus and his words seriously and hold his words close, so that the enemy does not swoop down like a bird plucking away seeds. I pray that the Holy Ghost will continue to inspire us all to recognize our own selfishness and how it allows lucifer and his to influence the world through us.

Hosea 4:2,3

2) By swearing, and lying, and killing, and stealing, and committing adultery, they break out, and blood toucheth blood.
3) Therefore shall the land mourn…

Finally, I pray we will see the poetry in motion in each of our lives, that is the Holy Ghost working hard through our selfishness to work all things out for good.

WHY PRAY

The biggest reason we pray that many fail to mention is simply because it acknowledges and recognizes God the Father. This is why Jesus himself starts out the Lord's prayer with this recognition and honor first.

Matthew 6:9,10
9) "After this manner therefore pray ye: Our Father which art in heaven, hallowed be thy name.
10) Thy kingdom come. Thy will be done in earth, as it is in heaven."

For what would it be like not to be recognized? Really think about what it feels like when nobody recognizes our achievements, our dreams or the fact that we even exist. How does it make us feel when we do so much for someone without getting so much as a thank you? How does it make us feel when others only seem to remember us when they need help, want something or want to make money from us? Sadly, this is not hard for many these days to imagine or remember. Now imagine how God the Father feels. We so often forget that we are made in his image and that he has feelings as well. A supreme being with all of his knowledge, wisdom and understanding. A creator with the source of all inspiration and he is forgotten and ignored by his own creation. Not only that, but he is cursed, mocked and blamed for every selfish thing that humanity was given the freedom to think up and act on.

So we pray first of all to give recognition to the one that created all things and is the source of all things good. Even Jesus acknowledges God as the Father and gives glory to his name right off the bat. We can never give God too much credit and glory for who he is and what he has done for us, unless it is just for show and we do not truly mean it. Just like anyone else, God loves to be truly recognized and it is the very least we can do.

Another reason we pray is because he listens and answers prayers. We are told that we have not because we ask not and asking requires praying.

James 4:2

2)   Ye lust, and have not: Ye kill, and desire to have, and cannot obtain: Ye fight and war, yet ye have not, because ye ask not.

Jesus lets us know that it is ok to ask for things and ask questions when he tells us to ask and we shall receive. He is especially pleased when we ask things of him for other people. Selfless acts are one of the traits that mark us as his and that makes him happy.

Matthew 7:7,8

7)   "Ask and it shall be given you: Seek, and ye shall find; Knock, and it shall be opened unto you:

8)   For every one that asketh receiveth; and he that seeketh findeth; and to him that knocketh it shall be opened."

We must remember that God the Father is not a genie that grants our every desire. This is how spoiled children are made that have no gratitude, or even know and appreciate where their gifts really come from. He grants our needs and answers prayers that bring him glory and furthers his kingdom. Our hearts and intentions have to be in line with his and only he knows where our hearts truly are. He does not cast his pearls before swine that only call out to him to use up his grace, only to turn back to evil ways when the road is clear, just to turn back again later with our hands out in times of desperation, again.

Matthew 7:6

6)   "Give not that which is holy unto the dogs, neither cast ye your pearls before swine, lest they trample them under their feet, and turn again and rend you."

James 4:3

3)   ye ask, and receive not, because ye ask amiss, that ye may consume it upon your lusts.

If we do not choose to continue walking with Jesus, our faith never grows to the faith of a mustard seed, being able to move mountains because we are always having to go through a process of getting ready in our hearts to receive. Each time we turn from God's path, we acquire more calluses that the spirit has to chip away again. Many of us have the same callus chipped away repeatedly. This only slows the plan of salvation making the job of the Holy Ghost harder, which is but one of lucifer's ways of causing problems. I heard it put well when I heard someone say, "If we stay ready; We ain't got to get ready."

Matthew 17:20

20)   "Because of your unbelief: For verily I say unto you, if ye have faith as a grain of mustard seed, ye shall say unto this mountain, remove hence to yonder place; and it shall remove; and nothing shall be impossible unto you."

Many would say that what Jesus suggests in this scripture is impossible. I would say it depends on one's perspective. I can understand one's doubt when we think within the limits we place due to our short lifespans. In our busy and fast paced lives, It is hard for many to think in terms of generations past our own existence. Many do not care about planting a tree that they know they themselves would never enjoy the shade from. In the over eight hundred thousand miles I have driven across the United States like Forrest Gump, I have witnessed mountains being moved from one place to another. It took about two years before anyone could see what was being done, but as the equipment worked on certain mountain sides along I80 and I40 in California and Nevada, the colors of the different formations started being visible from the interstates. Over the years to follow, one mountain would slowly go away. New mountains form as companies mine and deposit their unwanted dirt as ridges. Grass has grown on many over the years making it look natural even. In a generation or so, nobody will recognize the changes or even know that mountains were moved. Showing how even huge changes can go unnoticed if done slowly.

The scriptures are full of evidence that God hears our prayers and is eager to answer when our motives are pure and selfless.

Matthew 7:9-11

9) "or what man is there of you, whom if his son ask bread, will he give him a stone?
10) or if he ask a fish, will he give him a serpent?
11) If ye then, being evil, know how to give good gifts unto your children, how much more shall your Father which is in heaven give good things to them that ask him?

John 16:24

24) "Hitherto have ye asked nothing in my name: ask, and ye shall receive, that your joy may be full."

Philippians 4:6

6) Be careful for nothing; But in everything by prayer and supplication with thanksgiving let your requests be made known unto God.

James 5:13-15

13) Is any among you afflicted? Let him pray. Is any merry? Let him sing psalms.
14) Is any sick among you? Let him call for the elders of the church; And let them pray over him, anointing him with oil in the name of the Lord.
15) And the prayer of faith shall save the sick, and the Lord shall raise him up; and if he have committed sins, they shall be forgiven him.

1 Peter 3:12

12) For the eyes of the Lord are over the righteous, and his ears are open unto their prayers: But the face of the Lord is against them that do evil.

1 John 5:14,15

14) And this is the confidence that we have in him, that, if we ask any thing according to his will, he heareth us:
15) And if we know that he hear us, whatsoever we ask, we know that we have the petitions that we desired of him.

Psalms 66:17-20

17) I cried unto him with my mouth, and he was extolled with my tongue.
18) If I regard iniquity in my heart, the Lord will not hear me:
19) But verily God hath heard me; He hath attended to the voice of my prayer.
20) Blessed be God, which hath not turned away my prayer, nor his mercy from me.

Proverbs 15:29

29) The Lord is far from the wicked: But he heareth the prayer of the righteous.

Isaiah 65:24

24) And it shall come to pass, that before they call, I will answer; And while they are yet speaking, I will hear.

Jeremiah 29:12,13

12) Then shall ye call upon me, and ye shall go and pray unto me, and I will hearken unto you.
13) And ye shall seek me, and find me, when ye shall search for me with all your heart.

Jeremiah 33:3

3) Call unto me, and I will answer thee, and shew thee great and mighty things, which thou knowest not.

Numbers 21:5-9

5) And the people spake against God, and against Moses, wherefore have ye brought us up out of Egypt to die in the wilderness? For there is no bread, neither is there any water, and our soul loatheth this light bread.

6) And the Lord sent fiery serpents among the people, and they did bite the people; And much people of Israel died.

7) Therefore the people came to Moses, and said, we have sinned, for we have spoken against the Lord, and against thee; Pray unto the lord, that he take away the serpents from us. And Moses prayed for the people.

8) And the Lord said unto Moses, make thee a fiery serpent, and set it upon a pole: And it shall come to pass, that every one that is bitten, when he looketh upon it, shall live.

9) And Moses made a serpent of brass, and put it upon a pole, and it came to pass, that if a serpent had bitten any man, when he beheld the serpent of brass, he lived.

So let us also be eager to talk to God the Father through prayer. If anyone is having issues finding where to begin, remember that Jesus was our example in action and in words. Jesus was asked how we should pray and he gave us all a guideline or pattern to follow, along with a couple of don'ts. And again, the do nots draw out lucifer's system of thought because he will do them and teach others to do the same.

Matthew 6:5-13

5) "And when thou prayest, thou shalt not be as the hypocrites are: For they love to pray standing in synagogues and in the corners of the streets, that they may be seen of men. Verily I say unto you, they have their reward."

6) But thou, when thou prayest, enter into thy closet, and when thou hast shut thy door, pray to thy Father which is in secret: And thy Father which seeth in secret shall reward thee openly.

7) But when ye pray, use not vain repetitions, as the heathen do: For they think that they shall be heard for their much speaking.

8) Be not ye therefore like unto them: For your Father knoweth what things ye have need of before ye ask him.

9) After this manner therefore pray ye: Our Father which art in heaven, hallowed be thy name.

10) Thy kingdom come, thy will be done in earth as it is in heaven.

11) Give us this day our daily bread,

12) And forgive us our debts as we forgive our debtors.

13) And lead us not into temptation, but deliver us from evil: For thine is the kingdom, and the power, and the glory, forever, amen."

When there is no great need, this example is our pattern and guideline, because our Father knows our needs already. We are simply acknowledging him in all things and giving him thanks for it daily. God the Father is also eager to bless others when we choose to use our prayers on the needs of others. He is pleased to see us put away our own selfishness to use our petitions to bless others. This becomes easier to do when we become thankful and satisfied with only our needs. Our walk with Jesus one day at a time, helps us to see that our selfish wants are what blinds us to the needs of others. In the end, only God the Father knows the heart and intentions of each prayer. I pray that this helps anyone with questions or concerns about praying or how to pray. I pray that as we reach out to our Heavenly Father, we will do so in private so that our focus can be on connecting to our Father in heaven more than being seen praying. Our prayers can be seen in our lives if one knows to look for the fruits. Let us start each day as we open our eyes, giving God the Father the first fruits of our day in recognition and thanks for the very blessings of the love, life and time he grants each day. Then we can pray for each other as the day goes on. I pray that this would be a goal for every believer, and that our Father in heaven would bless us all for it. Finally, I pray that we would begin to see the poetry in motion through the network of prayers and how it helps the Holy Ghost in his mission to work all things for the good of all.

WHEN JESUS CALLS OUR NAME

In the middle of my forty day fast, I was driving over the mountains going into California on I40. I was about twenty days into my fast when the Holy Ghost started hitting me in waves. This is when I realized that now my cup was ready to be filled. I see a lot of homeless in my travels and I have always had a protective heart for abused children, but my empathy for the suffering and abuse began to be unbearable. I almost had to pull over twice on my way up I99 in California to deliver my camper. I prayed for the Holy Ghost to let me get my camper delivered before overwhelming me. I delivered the trailer and started back to Indiana on I80. As I was going over the mountains through Donner's pass and Truckee, The Holy Ghost started hitting me so hard that I had to stop. Luckily it was right at a good pull off that had river access. I went down to the river and was glad to see that nobody else was around because I began to weep uncontrollably for the homeless and his little ones being defiled all over the world. I have never been much of a crier, but I wept and cried out for the Father to do something for his children being harmed by wicked people. For him to send someone to help them. The very next moment after I cried out those words, the weight was gone and the Holy Ghost was there with his warm, loving comfort, giving the feeling that everything will be alright. I washed my face in the cold river and got back on the road feeling comforted that a prayer had been answered.

As I was driving down the mountain into Reno, I began to be inspired to carve something I have never attempted in my twenty five years of carving off and on. The Holy Ghost wanted me to carve a depiction of the crucifix. I did not know the scope of it, but I knew it would be used as a teaching aid for biblical lessons and somehow, it would help in the fight against the harming of his little ones. I found that Jesus is the master of killing multiple birds with one stone. I am learning not to question it.

Once I kind of realized what might be asked of me, I did what so many of us do when faced with what we see as too much responsibility; I argued with the Holy Ghost. I began first with that I was not good enough for a project like this. Almost all of my carving experience has been from carving while raising a young family. I was what I call a production carver, not an artist. I mass carved things that could be wholesaled and that was about it. I actually received the title of the bear machine because of the amount of little bears I could carve each day. I hadn't even carved much over the previous fifteen years due to chasing oilfield money. I could have definitely counted numerous others way more qualified. The Holy Ghost impressed on me that those were the reasons for why me and I did not know if the Holy Ghost just insulted me or if I insulted myself.

So I went to the next argument, what wood to use for a project like this. The only thing I could think of that would be adequate enough was redwood. The only wood that could have been a sapling while Jesus walked the earth, and still usable today as old growth wood. I thought I had won when I asked where I would get such a big piece of redwood. Redwood was already getting unreasonably expensive when my wife and I moved back to Texas from the redwoods about sixteen years before this. My heart sank when the reply was, "why do you think you have been carrying all that redwood around for the last sixteen years, moving it from place to place with no desire to touch it"? You see, before my wife and I moved back to Texas to plant some roots, We lived in northern California in the redwoods on hwy 101. In our early marriage while raising our first child, we moved from Texas to California to get closer to the redwoods because in my opinion, redwood is the best carving wood. We followed the competition circuit for a few years on the west coast and met a lot of really blessed and good hearted people. Being in a prodigal son position, we met wolves also that only saw how much I could produce. Our kids finally got to the age that we felt it was time to go home and plant some roots. Plus, we were young and gullible and got involved with a wolf so we thought it best to cut ties and just go home. My wife stuck by my side those years living mostly in a small camper. So when we returned home I went into the oilfield so she could stay home in a house to be there for our children. Before moving back, I had bought a bunch of old growth redwood blocks to take back to Texas. Only, I got caught up in chasing oilfield money and never did anything with it. We just moved it around from place to place for about sixteen years.

I still thought I had the upper hand because I quickly said, "But they are all in different sized pieces". Again the Holy Ghost had an answer. The inspiration hit me that the different pieces would represent the lesson taught by the Apostle Paul in 1 Corinthians 12:22. How no one body part is more important than another, and what happens when the body parts forget their place and how to work together for the profit of all. It seemed that the Holy Ghost had thought of everything already.

Running out of arguments, I grasped out with my fear of doing faces. To me, faces are complex. Especially for someone who had only tried a couple of times in their whole career. Yet again, the Holy Ghost had an answer. I was to put a mirror in the place of the face that would speak differently to each person, depending on where they are in heart, life and intent. I was to use the caption, "because nobody truly understands until it's them".

The last fear I could use was my fear of how it would be received. I began to imagine all of the harsh judges saying that I was creating a false idol and that I was doing it for myself. The Holy Ghost comforted me and said to not fear what is conceived in the spirit, then gave me two scriptures; Numbers 21:4-9 and John 3:14,15. Numbers 21 is a story of what happens when we turn our eyes from God the Father and disobey his commands. We become plagued by snakes and their venom kills us. This is a lesson for us today as we see the infestation of snakes in the hen house eating the eggs of the people. We are slowly dying by the selfish venom of these snakes that our ignorance has let in. Only by looking at the fiery serpent could they be saved. Many of us know John 3:16. So much so that we let it dwarf the previous two verses that point to the foreshadowing of Numbers 21. Jesus is telling us that to save ourselves from the selfishness caused by that old serpent's bite, we have to turn our eyes back to Jesus, the cross and the examples he left for us. To his teachings that he knew would be echoed throughout all of time. My lesson was that God did not have Moses make a false idol but a tool to focus his people's attention back to him as well as test their ability to obey and remember.

At this point I had no other argument than I did not sign up for this. It was at this point I knew God the Father had a sense of humor as I heard my own voice crying out for the Lord to do something. After a moment of shock, then admiration, I began to think back on how perfectly he timed so many things for this moment. The uncanny way my wife and I met, which is a story of its own because I married into the carving world. All of the meetings and experiences that would not have been if even one thing happened differently. I began to see the poetry in motion.

Now this part of the story I enjoy sharing, mainly because I really did not know when the Lord would bring me home for the project he commissioned me to do. Much less how I was going to afford to stay home for the time it would take to complete it, because I kind of saw it as an unspoken test. After fourteen years of sitting still and working in the oilfield, we had acquired debt from reaching for too much. This problem is so common that I do not feel the need to explain much on that part. So we did not currently have the ability to take off for too long, but, my current lesson was to trust in the Lord one day at a time.

As I drove across the country in March of 2020, I began to feel the Holy Ghost tug at me like it was getting close to go home, only I was still worrying over how without putting ourselves behind. Then something happened that surprised me, Covid started "hitting". I spent the rest of March and the first part of April delivering campers across America and personally seeing how America reacted to a "pandemic". As I traveled, the Holy Ghost had me pay attention to the discrepancies from what the media was saying and what was really going on across America. Regardless, I could not believe that the Lord was going to stop the world so I could go home to do this commissioned piece. Because of Covid, we were able to defer enough payments that allowed me to come home for a two week quarantine, even though I never got sick. This is why I call this piece my "quarantine project". Once again showing how God the Father turns what is meant for evil, for good. I continued to be in awe of the poetry in motion that I was witnessing as I learned to slow down to a one day at a time mentality. I was witnessing the Holy Ghost at work and what it means when Jesus calls our name and we see a purpose.

ONE DAY AT A TIME

    The funny thing about lost things, they most often times end up being found in a spot that we passed several times in our search. Many times we realize after finding the lost object that we looked at it, but never really saw it. I myself have been a part of a group looking for something that ended up right in front of us the whole time. In our haste and impatience, we do not realize that we blind ourselves. We move so fast in our search for something lost, we often continue to overlook the very thing we seek to find. It has been my experience that we usually find what we are looking for after we slow down, take that deep breath and really start looking with full intent. Often enough, it is when we finally get on our knees and see things from a different angle. Mostly because until this point, we are only searching with half intent. This is usually when the lights hit it just right and because we are on our knees, we see it. It just took the right angle and perspective.
    When I was starting this Jesus piece, I was faced with having to look in the very mirror that this piece asks others to look into. To be honest, It almost broke me. I am not too proud to admit it. It took me a good part of day one to clean up all of the beer bottles and cans I had acquired. When I thought I was done and I learned my lesson on not letting things pile up in my life, I had to ask myself, if God wanted to use any of us today, how much cleaning up would we need to do before he can even start? Would we even hear him calling to us over the noise and mess we let into our lives? Have we taken in good things for him to use or things that we have to fight over in our own heads as we get older? Certain filth we let into our minds by the things we choose to experience and the things we let our eyes see and our ears to hear, is like the venom in a bee sting or an acid trip, It never leaves our body. It continues to circulate, adding up until it comes back to haunt us later in our lives. Usually when

we have straightened up and are trying to do good, and no, I have never done acid. I learn from the mistakes of others, or I try. Certain things we allowed ourselves to see we struggle with as we are trying to be faithful to both God and our loved ones. This was my first lesson on going one day at a time. Not to move so fast that we miss today's love, life and time worrying about tomorrow or yesterday. This is how things pile up and sneak up on us in the end. Realizing this definitely makes one understand why God's people of old seemed so stern and strict to us today. They understood what constantly saying, "oh it's ok, it won't hurt anything", will do to a culture over generations of time.

    Into the afternoon of the first day, I thought I was done and sat back looking at all of the trash bags filled with beer bottles and cans. Then I looked in all of the nooks and crannies and began to weep. The realization of how far I had let myself go really hit me. I thought for sure that the Lord chose the wrong sinner for this project. The Holy Ghost hit me with that warm, loving and patient feeling that everything is ok, helping me to understand that it is more about this realization and understanding than ever becoming good enough to start. That it is about coming to the understanding that we cannot do it on our own. That trying to do it on our own is what put us in our positions to begin with. If we try to wait until we have cleaned up all of our messes, we would never start. With that, I was inspired to begin the project.

    Now I have to admit, I had never really done a piece like this before. All of my experience was in doing production carving to make a living. I mainly did animals and most of those were character bears that are unrealistic looking. I started with the cross, which I was inspired to start on the ground. All of the wood I had carried around for sixteen years was in different shapes and sizes, but that is what the Holy Ghost wanted. So I was to carve body parts from different pieces of redwood that I had for some reason carried around for 16 years, and put them together as the body of Christ. I did not remember the reason until after it was completed because I was scared of the task. I didn't even know where to start. All I saw at the end of the first day was a wooden cross on the ground with several pieces of wood laid out on top. The Holy Ghost said that was good for the day so I gave thanks for the day and went inside. The next day I woke up, gave thanks to our Heavenly Father for the love, life and time of the new day and said my morning prayer after looking at the start of this piece, not knowing what to do. The Holy Ghost answered by inspiring me to start with the head, so I spent the day carving the head. I am usually scared to do faces but I knew I was getting out easy on this one since I was putting a mirror in place of a face. While working on the head, I noticed myself occasionally looking at the other blocks of wood already feeling inferior for the job because I could not see it yet. I could almost feel a slap on the back of my head to pull my eyes back to the task for the day, with the Holy Ghost saying, "not yet". I ended the day in thanks with the head complete and the rest mocking me.

 The next day after prayer, I began to see the shape of the torso form where the head touched the block of wood that would be the torso. I carved along until I got stumped. I could not see where to go next. After a quick silent prayer, the Holy Ghost inspired me to lift the head of the cross up about two feet. While I was on my knees blocking up the cross, I noticed I could see what to do next. I spent the day carving the torso using my son as a model to get the proportions right, all the while I was still taking glances at the other blocks, not able to see them yet. Again, the feeling or thought of a slap and, "not yet". I ended the day with thanks and started to look forward to the next day.

 Day four started the same, prayer and seeing the arms and hands take shape. Again, I get stumped halfway through the day and I am inspired to lift the head of the cross another two feet. From this perspective, I was able to see and finish the arms and things I did not see on the torso. At the end of this day, even though I was giving thanks, I was still worrying myself over not being able to see the legs or feet yet, and yet again, slap, "not yet".

 The next day I started the same, with prayer and thanks.

Only this time I could not really see where to start. I went into the house for a bit and my wife and I got into a small argument. She went into the living room on the other side of the house and I flopped onto the bed like a spoiled child. I proceeded to tell Jesus that if he really wanted me to work on this piece, my wife was going to have to apologize to me. For some reason I was acting like an artist that could not work or be inspired while being upset. While we are not to test the Lord in questioning his authority, we are allowed and encouraged to test instructions to be certain it is of the Lord.

Judges 6:36-40

36) And Gideon said unto God, if thou wilt save Israel by mine hand, as thou hast said,

37) Behold, I will put a fleece of wool in the floor; And if the dew be on the fleece only, and it be dry upon all the earth beside, then shall I know that thou wilt save Israel by mine hand, as thou hast said.

38) And it was so: For he rose up early on the morrow, and thrust the fleece together, and wringed the dew out of the fleece, a bowl full of water.

39) And Gideon said unto God, let not thine anger be hot against me, and I will speak but this once: Let me prove, I pray thee, but this once with the fleece; Let it now be dry only upon the fleece, and upon all the ground let there be dew.

40) And God did so that night: For it was dry upon the fleece only, and there was dew on all the ground.

My wife believes in God and has a huge heart but she is not religious, meaning she is like so many others including myself at one time, she does not trust a book written by man's hand. Settling into what I thought would be a day off, My wife came into the room about 2 minutes later. She gave me a hug, apologized and said, "If the Lord wants you to do this piece, you need to get back to work". All I could do was hug her, tell her I love her and go back outside knowing I would probably pay for that feat. As I approached the project, I was inspired to raise the cross up almost all of the way, leaning it against a live oak branch, and there it was. I could see the legs as if they were already carved. I ended the day in thanks and for once, not worried about tomorrow and the making of the feet. No slap this time, but still a faint, "not yet".

Day six I started with prayer and an eagerness for the day knowing the project was almost done. I easily knocked out the feet and other touch ups I could now see from this perspective. It was at this point the question hit me as to how I was to hold all of the pieces together. As a perfectionist at times, I wanted to hide the seams of the connecting body parts the best I could. This is when the Holy Ghost inspired me to make the seams visible so everyone sees that the piece is not all of one piece of wood, then remove the rods I was using and replace them with magnets, which are to represent the spirit that holds the body of Christ together. Most of us have played with magnets as a kid and we know what happens when we get our magnets backwards. God the Father is the constant, always trying to draw us near. It is our magnets that get flipped around by our selfishness that pushes us away from him. Jesus is teaching us how to flip our magnets back around in all aspects of our lives and society. All so we can see what heaven on earth looks like after the body of Christ comes together. Because of the magnets, I can remove different body parts easily, helping to explain visibly the lesson both Jesus and the Apostle Paul teaches about a body and their many parts. How no one body part is more important than another. All of the inspirations during my forty day fast hit me. The mirror, the different body parts and the magnets, it was all to make this piece a teaching aid for the biblical lessons that we all need to learn and remember to make it through what is coming. To help many with putting certain things back into perspective. It taught me that we are never given the whole recipe for many reasons, one being that we all are bad about trying to deviate, thinking that we can do things better. I gave thanks as I pondered on Jesus's lessons and his message to all, even his church, through this piece.

After my prayer the next day, I moved the piece to stand by the highway as I started putting the finish coats on. This was Easter Sunday of 2020. The inspiration for this project and my forty day fast taking place in January of 2020. While there are many lessons to be learned, the main one that stood out during the making of this piece was that we all need to learn to slow back down to one day at a time. I realized how much we blind ourselves from the blessings he wants to give us each day, by worrying and fearing about tomorrow and regretting things of yesterday. He gives us the love, life and time we need for each day, but we constantly bankrupt ourselves by trying to borrow from tomorrow or spending what is meant for today on the past problems of yesterday. Do we each need a slap on the back of the head and a "not yet"? I learned that the start to a fix is to slow down to one day at a time, which should always start on our knees in prayer, actually asking and searching. Starting with the cross and Jesus at the head of any body. Only from there do we see our perspective rise as we raise the cross.

    A few months later, as "Covid" was "really hitting", My family had to move like so many others had to in the middle of a pandemic. My wife and I were suddenly living in our one ton trucks as we both delivered campers across the United States. This eventually led to the Holy Ghost inspiring me to travel the U.S. with this piece mounted in my truck, since we just happened to be blessed with the job and equipment to do just that. Which has blessed both my wife and me with meeting many fellow believers, as well as with having many encounters and experiences over three hundred thousand miles traveling like Forrest Gump, gathering often with believers from all over, reminding everyone we can of the story of Moses and his people in Numbers 21:5-9 and Jesus's words in John 3:14,15. Showing others what we as a nation need to put our eyes back on if we want to survive the selfish bite of that old serpent and his snakes that are in the hen house.

    My prayer is that as we get closer to the end, we as a nation would turn our eyes away from lucifer and the things of this world that are corrupt. That we turn our eyes back to Jesus and his words and actions. That we as a nation, Fall to our knees and let the cross and the light of Christ raise our perspectives, to help us find what we lost and are moving too fast to see. May the Holy Ghost continue to work his poetry in motion in each of our lives, waking us up to the selfishness of humanity and the need for the cure to this disease that is our selfishness. Finally, I pray we learn the lessons of the bible on returning to one day at a time and the importance of remaining there.

THE CASE FOR THE SEVENTH DAY

First off, I am not Seventh Day Adventist. The reason I call it the case for the seventh day is because like a court case, this subject is serious enough to really look at all of the evidence whether for or against. Too many these days accept a change without ever asking questions or even looking for proper proof for a change. We sometimes are too eager to follow a change and refuse to look at evidence in fear that we may learn that we have been fooled. Foolery is the specialty of lucifer as we see in the case of Eve all the way to the Scribes and the Pharisees. What gave lucifer such a strong foothold is too many think we today are infallible and the infiltration of lucifer's system of thought stopped with the Scribes and Pharisees, and the ones guilty of this change were the only ones with the holy scriptures for many generations. It was a long while before "common" people were able to read for themselves, able to see what things were taught and made a habit for people that actually go against the very commands and instructions of Jesus. Once again, lucifer was infecting the minds of religious leaders to be guilty of the very things Jesus rebuked the Scribes and Pharisees for doing. Changing laws and placing added burdens to worship that makes it almost impossible for his children to serve. Ultimately the goal of lucifer is to place himself in Jesus's place and trick us into doing the same. Hopefully by looking through the evidence, we can answer some questions about the sabbath day. Like how important was this day to God our creator? Do his chosen people still observe it today? Did God the Father or Jesus himself ever say it would be changed and who changed it and why? Since the evidence for the seventh day follows a timeline for these answers, I will start at the beginning with the creation of all things.

Genesis 2:2,3

2) And on the seventh day God ended his work which he had made; And he rested on the seventh day from all his work which he had made.

3) And God blessed the seventh day, and sanctified it: Because that in it he had rested from all his work which God created and made.

One thing I would like to point out is that God always refers to the days as numbers; First day, second day, seventh day. The names that we know as days are not biblical and raises the question of where did the names come from? The Romans were the ones who named the days of the week. They chose to name them after the sun, moon and five other planets that all were the names of the false gods they worshiped.

With the change from numbers to names of false gods aside, it is clear that God rested on the seventh day. He even sanctified it and made it holy. God the Father, our creator, considered the seventh day Sabbath important enough to have Moses and his rescued people abide by it in the wilderness. After being slaves to the Egyptians for so long, God's people had to be trained how to trust in God again and re-trained in how to do it one day at a time. They no longer knew how to live one day at a time trusting in their creator. God even uses manna from heaven to teach and train them in the rest of the seventh day Sabbath. Many forget about Egypt enslaving God's chosen to build their empire, making God's people work on and eventually forget God's day of rest after so many generations. Then wonder why the Egyptians or their ancestors were plagued by slavery themselves later in the future. Sins of the parents passing to future generations due to the system of thought of lucifer being taught and repeated each generation.

Exodus 16:4,5

4) Then said the Lord unto Moses, behold, I will rain bread from heaven for you; And the people shall go out and gather a certain rate every day, that I may prove them, whether they will

walk in my law, or no.
5)   And it shall come to pass, that on the sixth day they shall prepare that which they bring in: And it shall be twice as much as they gather daily.

Exodus 16:22-27

22)   And it came to pass, that on the sixth day they gathered twice as much bread, two omers for one man: and all the rulers of the congregation came and told Moses:
23)   And he said unto them, this is that which the Lord hath said, to morrow is the rest of the holy Sabbath unto the Lord: Bake that which ye will bake to day, and seethe that ye will seethe, and that which remaineth over lay up for you to be kept until the morning.
24)   And they laid up till the morning, as Moses bade: And it did not stink, neither was there any worms therein.
25)   And Moses said, eat that to day; For to day is a Sabbath unto the Lord: To day ye shall not find it in the field.
26)   Six days ye shall gather it; but on the seventh day, which is the Sabbath, in it there shall be none.
27)   And it came to pass, that there went out some of the people on the seventh day for to gather, and they found none.

Nothing new under the sun. Even then the selfishness of humanity was showing as they were provided all the food they needed, yet some still went to try and gather more. Whether it was out of greed, gluttony or some other selfish sin, it was something that God the Father was trying to work out of them. He was teaching them how to enter into his rest. So far it seems that God the Father considers the seventh day Sabbath important since he himself not only sanctified it and set it aside as holy, but also spent 40 years teaching his chosen people to remember and to observe it. It can be seen in these verses that God uses our observance of the seventh day as a test of our ability to obey his law. Even his chosen people still had trouble with unbelief, because there were those that still went looking for manna on the seventh day after being told there would be none.

They even had trouble following other orders because they were told to only gather for each day what they needed, not wanted. Even back then we had trouble separating our wants from our needs. The leftovers many hoped to save were all rotted and filled with worms and stank by morning. In their case, their selfish sin of untrust that God would take care of them pointed them out due to the rotting smell.

Exodus 16:19-21

19) And Moses said, let no man leave of till the morning.
20) Notwithstanding they hearkened not unto Moses; But some of them left of it until the morning, and it bred worms, and stank: and Moses was wroth with them.
21) And they gathered it every morning, every man according to his eating: And when the sun waxed hot, it melted.

Exodus 16:28

28) And the Lord said unto Moses, how long refuse ye to keep my commandments and my laws?

Does this sound like something that he intends to change or even let man change? Even before the ten commandments were given to Moses on stone tablets, God considered the proper observance of the seventh day Sabbath of rest a law and commandment. The proper observance of the sabbath day sets us apart as his people, showing that we trust in him and remember why he rested; Because he created all things in six days and he himself rested on the seventh day, making God the Father the maker of the proper work week and the proper reset for a people. Remembering and honoring the seventh day not only shows God that we trust him, but that we remember and honor his story and who he is, our creator. It is also another way that we acknowledge him and his authority over us as his creations. Again, God saw it important enough to make it a commandment and law written in stone. Not only that, but also thought it important enough to also give the most description of it among all ten of his commandments, as well as starting it off with a warning to remember it.

Exodus 20:8-11

8) Remember the Sabbath day, to keep it holy.
9) Six days shalt thou labour, and do all thy work:
10) But the seventh day is the sabbath of the Lord thy God: In it thou shalt not do any work, thou, nor thy son, nor thy daughter, thy manservant, nor thy maidservant, nor thy cattle, nor thy stranger that is within thy gates:
11) For in six days the Lord made heaven and earth, the sea, and all that in them is, and rested the seventh day: Wherefore the Lord blessed the Sabbath day, and hallowed it.

We are often good at looking for loopholes around God's laws. Our selfish nature is always at work to excuse why we disobey God. He makes it clear on what day the Sabbath is and what we are not to do. Notice he starts the Sabbath commandment out with remember? He knows the adversary and his desire to undermine God's authority, his desire to replace God. Lucifer has been doing this since before the garden and is still calling God a liar, trying to convince us that God is not serious about the things he says and commands. God repeatedly lets Moses know the importance of the seventh day Sabbath to him, and how important it should be to each of us.

Exodus 31:13-18

13) Speak thou also unto the children of Israel, saying, verily, my Sabbaths ye shall keep: For it is a sign between me and you throughout your generations; That ye may know that I am the Lord that doth sanctify you.
14) Ye shall keep the Sabbath therefore; for it is holy unto you: Everyone that defileth it shall surely be put to death: For whosoever doth any work therein, that soul shall be cut off from among his people.
15) Six days may work be done; But in the seventh is the Sabbath of rest, holy to the Lord: Whosoever doeth any work in the Sabbath day, he shall surely be put to death.

16) Wherefore the children of Israel shall keep the Sabbath, to observe the Sabbath <u>throughout their generations, for a perpetual covenant.</u>

17) <u>It is a sign between me and the children of Israel for ever:</u> For six days the Lord made heaven and earth, <u>and on the seventh day he rested, and was refreshed.</u>

18) And he gave unto Moses, when he made an end of communing with him upon Mount Si'nai, two tablets of testimony, tablets of stone, written with the finger of God.

    Even though I am trying to stay in order, I will however take a moment to address at this time where some might say that this covenant was for the children of Israel only, or for the Jew only. The Apostle Paul makes it clear that we become a Jew in heart when we believe and follow the law and therefore become a seed of Abraham. This is how Abraham could have children that numbered like the stars. We become a Jew in heart by the blood of Jesus. All who believe in Jesus are reconciled together as a seed of Abraham, as one of the many children of God that make up the body of Christ. Not to mention that being put to death meant that they were cast out and shunned. They were then considered spiritually dead. They were seen as dead until they did what was needed to return to the body. Jesus himself points out this way of seeing unbelievers as dead, or as he means, spiritually dead when recruiting a follower. Many do not pay attention to Jesus's answer to this man who asks if he can go bury his dad first before following him. Jesus tells this man to let the dead, (spiritually dead), bury their dead. He is telling him to let those that truly do not believe in his promises and commands bury the dead, for they spend too much time on grieving due to a lack of belief in his words and actions.

Genesis 15:5

5) And he brought him forth abroad, and said, look now toward heaven, and tell the stars, if thou be able to number them: and he said unto him, so shall thy seed be.

Romans 2: 28,29

28) For he is not a Jew, which is one outwardly; Neither is that circumcision, which is outward in the flesh:
29) But he is a Jew, which is one inwardly; and circumcision is that of the heart, in the spirit, and not in the letter; Whose praise is not of flesh, but of God.

Luke 9:59,60

59) And he said unto another, "follow me". But he said, Lord, suffer me first to go and bury my father.
60) Jesus said unto him, "let the dead bury their dead; but go thou and preach the kingdom of God.

With that aside, God spends a lot of time reminding his people to remember and honor the Sabbath day of rest. He makes sure to instill to his people that it is on the seventh day and that it is and will always be a sign between creator and his chosen created, a test for his people to see if we remember and honor his perpetual covenant throughout all generations. Or do we forget and become lazy and selfish enough to allow lucifer's system of thought to trick us into changing it to suit our selfish desires? All throughout the old testament the Lord's chosen have been instructed to observe the seventh day of rest. They took it seriously enough to close the city gates so merchants would not defile the city by exchanging money on God's day of rest. One could say that not being able to remember and honor this first command that he ever taught his people is why cities see so much evil. But it is easier to blame many other things when following lucifer's system of thought.

Nehemiah 13:18-21

18) Did not your fathers thus, and did not our God bring all this evil upon us, and upon this city? Yet ye bring more wrath upon Israel by profaning the Sabbath.
19) And it came to pass, that when the gates of Jerusalem began to be dark before the Sabbath, I commanded that the gates should be shut, and charged that they should not be opened till after the Sabbath: And some of my servants set I at the gates, that

there should no burden be brought in on the Sabbath day.
20) So the merchants and sellers of any kind of ware lodged without Jerusalem once or twice.
21) Then I testified against them, and said unto them, why lodge ye about the wall? If ye do so again, I will lay hands on you. From that time forth came they no more on the Sabbath.

Jeremiah 17:19-23,27

19) Thus said the Lord unto me: Go and stand in the gate of the children of the people, whereby the kings of Judah come in, and by the which they go out, and in all the gates of Jerusalem;
20) And say unto them, hear ye the word of the Lord, ye kings of Judah, and all Judah, and all the inhabitants of Jerusalem, that enter in by these gates.
21) Thus saith the Lord; Take heed to yourselves, and bear no burden on the Sabbath day, nor bring it in by the gates of Jerusalem;
22) Neither carry forth a burden out of your houses on the Sabbath day, neither do ye any work, but hallow ye the Sabbath day, as I commanded your fathers.
23) But they obeyed not, neither inclined their ear, but made their neck stiff, that they might not hear, nor receive instruction.
27) But if ye will not hearken unto me to hallow the Sabbath day, and not to bear a burden, even entering in at the gates of Jerusalem on the Sabbath day; Then will I kindle a fire in the gates thereof, and it shall devour the palaces of Jerusalem, and it shall not be quenched.

God the Father was serious enough about the Sabbath day to not only command us to remember it, but to also warn us. God warns us all through a vision he gave to Daniel. The vision warns of a system of thought that is led by a position of authority that gains great influence over kings, and will think it has the authority to change the times and laws of God himself. As it arises and transforms after the death of Jesus, we can almost see lucifer's system of thought move from the

Scribes and Pharisees to this new system because it repeats the same mistakes, as well as some new ones that disobey Jesus's simplest of commands.

Daniel 7:24,25

24) And the ten horns out of this kingdom are ten kings that shall arise: And another shall rise after them; and he shall be diverse from the first, and he shall subdue three kings,

25) And he shall speak great words against the most high, and shall wear out the saints of the most high, and think to change times and laws: And they shall be given into his hands until a time and times and the dividing of times.

The stories in the book of Daniel of the lion's den and the fiery furnace teach and remind us that there is always lucifer's system of thought working in the background, using wicked and selfish men in high positions to attack those that try to obey God's commands. They will twist laws to not only line their own pockets, but to trick God's people into going against God's truths. All to get rid of them because they know that God blesses everything his true followers do which usually points out the flaws in those that are corrupt. Exactly like what was done to Jesus.

So this position of power ran by men is diverse, different from previous ones in that it will have influence and much control over kings and rulers. "He" will sit and act as a form of king. "He" will believe that his system of thought has the authority to change God's times and laws, starting with God's first one from creation, to observe, remember and honor the seventh day Sabbath of rest. And the saints are worn out over time because they were tricked once again into forgetting not only when and how to enter into his rest, but the benefits of that rest to be rejuvenated for each new week. The saints are running on empty because of this trickery. Lucifer, from the beginning has been all about undermining the authority and rule of God the Father. Lucifer does not need to work hard at tripping God's people into bars and nightclubs. Our own selfish nature does a good job at that. Lucifer has spent thousands of years trying to twist God's word in order to fool masses, not just a few here and there. Oddly enough, he still uses very close to the same line he used with Eve in the beginning to call God a liar, "Oh, he wasn't serious when he said that," sound familiar? One can almost hear the venom off of those words. Saying that God or Jesus were not serious about their words and commands is speaking great words against the most high, since all of their commands pertain to our forgiveness, salvation and our way home to the Father, which they never joked about. Thinking to have the authority to change the seventh day of rest is thinking to change times and laws and is exactly why God said to remember it. He did not say to change it and teach future generations of his children to ignore then forget about it all together.

    Now that we have seen an undeniable case for the commanded seventh day of rest throughout the old testament, along with a brief look at our culprit of change, what does the new testament say about the seventh day of rest and see if his chosen still observed it. Did Jesus himself observe the seventh day Sabbath or even speak of another day? Afterall, he was our perfect example to follow.

Luke 4:16
16)   And he came to Nazareth, where he had been brought up: And, as his custom was, he went into the synagogue on the Sabbath day, and stood up for to read.

Luke 6:6
6)   And it came to pass also on another Sabbath, that he entered into the synagogue and taught: and there was a man whose right hand was withered.

Matthew 12:10-13
10)   And, behold, there was a man which had his hand withered. And they asked him, saying, is it lawful to heal on the Sabbath days? That they might accuse him.

11) And he said unto them, "What man shall there be among you, that shall have one sheep, and if it fall into a pit on the Sabbath day, will he not lay hold on it, and lift it out?
12) How much then is a man better than a sheep? Wherefore it is lawful to do well on the Sabbath days".
13) Then saith he to the man, "stretch forth thine hand". And he stretched it forth; And it was restored whole, like as the other.

Acts 17:2

2) And Paul, as his manner was, went in unto them, and three
Sabbath days reasoned with them out of the scriptures.

Acts 18:4

4) And he reasoned in the synagogue every Sabbath, and persuaded the Jews and the Greeks.

Hebrews 4:1-11

1) Let us therefore fear, lest, a promise being left us of entering into his rest, any of you should seem to come short of it.
2) For unto us was the gospel preached, as well as unto them: But the word preached did not profit them, not being mixed with faith in them that heard it.
3) For we which have believed do enter into rest, as he said, as I have sworn in my wrath, if they shall enter into my rest: Although the works were finished from the foundation of the world.
4) For he spake in a certain place of the seventh day on this wise, and God did rest the seventh day from all his works.
5) And in this place again, if they shall enter into my rest.
6) Seeing therefore it remaineth that some must enter therein, and they to whom it was first preached entered not in because of unbelief:
7) Again, he limiteth a certain day, saying in David, to day, after so long a time; As it is said, to day if ye will hear his voice, harden not your hearts.

8) For if Jesus had given them rest, then would he not have spoken of another day?
9) There remaineth therefore a rest to the people of God.
10) For he that is entered into his rest, he also hath ceased from his own works, as God did from his.
11) Let us labour therefore to enter into that rest, lest any man fall after the same example of unbelief.

Jesus told the followers in his day to listen to the religious leaders who sit in Moses's seat. Even they still observed the seventh day of rest commanded by God from the beginning of creation. Jesus's problem with the Sabbath day of rest was only that the religious leaders added rules for the day not set by God, making it almost impossible for his people to observe properly. Their goal was to keep the people burdened so that they would continue to buy sacrifices, which became a form of selling salvation. It was through these added rules that they tried to trap Jesus so that they could discredit him and get rid of him.

Matthew 23:1-4

1) Then spake Jesus to the multitude, and to his disciples,
2) Saying, "The Scribes and the Pharisees sit in Moses's seat:
3) All therefore whatsoever they bid you observe, that observe and do; But do not ye after their works: For they say, and do not.
4) For they bind heavy burdens and grieves to be borne, and lay them on men's shoulders; But they themselves will not move them with one of their fingers".

If we read the original instructions for the Sabbath day, The seventh day of rest, there is no rule for not walking or healing on the Sabbath day. Notice also, Neither God himself or Jesus ever called the sabbath day of rest a day of worship. Nowhere in the entire bible did they ever dedicate one single day as a day of worship. We are to worship everyday by remembering and honoring his commands to be kind and forgiving, showing to each other the very same mercy we ask for. He did however set one day aside as a day of rest and said to remember that day. The added rules came as lucifer infected the religious leaders with greed after seeing how much money, power and control could be obtained through the sins of the people, so they added burdens not of God to increase those sins that had to have sacrifices to pay for. Jesus says plainly that it is ok to do well. God said it simply when he called it a day of rest from work. A rest from our gathering and our heavy day to day burdens. We are simply not supposed to work for money or personal gain, and this includes household chores like cooking, cleaning and carrying heavy loads. Not only are we not supposed to do any work, whoever we have under us all of the way down to our ox and mule are to rest on the seventh day. How many "Christian" businesses build their wealth by making their laborers work on the proper Sabbath day of rest? All throughout the old testament and the new, the seventh day Sabbath has been remembered and observed even by Jesus. Not once does Jesus say or imply that the Sabbath day of rest was going to be changed or done away with. We are even warned against a change and commanded to remember it and to keep it holy. Not to mention we are told to be on the lookout for those that would think to change God's times and laws, all while defaming the most high's words by saying he was not serious.

    Jesus himself said that he did not come to change the law, but to fulfill it. He did not come to change the Sabbath day, but to fulfill the law of sacrifice needed to pay the debt for the selfishness of all humanity. To take away the ability of corrupted men to control and sell salvation as we see done in the past and in today's society. Ending the need for any other sacrifice for those that believe in Jesus and his ultimate sacrifice. This is why Jesus said on the cross that it is finished. With his innocent death by his own people filled with pride and greed, he fulfilled the law of sacrifice and met the qualifications for equivalent exchange.

Matthew 5:17-19

17) "Think not that I am come to destroy the law, or the prophets: I am not come to destroy, but to fulfill.
18) For verily I say unto you, till heaven and earth pass, one jot or one tittle shall in no wise pass from the law, till all be fulfilled.
19) Whosoever therefore shall break one of these least commandments, and shall teach men so, he shall be called the least in the kingdom of heaven: But whosoever shall do and teach them, the same shall be called great in the kingdom of heaven".

Many try to say that Jesus's raising on the first day changed the Sabbath day that we were told to remember. Yet nowhere does it say that Jesus came out of the tomb saying that his death and resurrection did away with the observance of the seventh day Sabbath. Nowhere did Jesus speak of another day. Notice what day Mary was coming to prepare the body of Jesus and why. She came on the first day because she could not do any work on the seventh day of rest. Do we not really think she would have liked to prepare his body on the seventh day? Nowhere is Mary told to not observe the seventh day of rest anymore. The very death, burial and resurrection of Jesus observed the rules of the seventh day Sabbath of rest. His body stayed resting over the Sabbath day, keeping the day holy. After the Sabbath day, he arose changed and rejuvenated and appeared to Mary because it was the first day for work to be done.

John 20:1

1) The first day of the week cometh Mary Magdalene early, When it was yet dark, unto the sepulchre, and seeth the stone taken away from the sepulchre.

Jesus never even told his apostles that his resurrection changed any observance of the seventh day of rest. So far, even up to the ascension of Jesus into heaven, there is nothing but thousands of years of solid evidence for the case of the seventh day observance, as well as its importance as a sign between God and his people that God said would last unchanged throughout all time and generations, and Jesus himself said would not change or pass away until <u>all</u> is fulfilled. Jesus did not say on the cross that all was fulfilled, but that it was finished. The law of sacrifice was finished by his death and resurrection. The plan of salvation will not be fulfilled until his second coming.

    The only assumed evidence for a change is a baseless assumption that stems from the fact that the apostles started gathering on the first day. This is where I have to remind that there is a huge difference between the Sabbath day of rest and merely gathering for various reasons, which is all the apostles were doing. We can gather six days a week and it would not do away with the commandment of the seventh day of rest. We were commanded to gather often and to not forsake the gatherings but still does not do away with the commanded Sabbaths.

Acts 20:7

7)   And upon the first day of the week, when the disciples came together <u>to break bread</u>, Paul preached unto them, ready to depart on the morrow; And continued his speech until midnight.

1 Corinthians 16:2

2)   Upon the first day of the week let every one of you lay by him in store, as God hath prospered him, that there be no gatherings when I come.

John 20:19

19)   Then the same day at evening, being the first day of the week, when doors were shut <u>where the disciples were assembled for fear of the Jews,</u> came Jesus and stood in the midst, and saith unto them, "peace be unto you".

Hebrews 10:25

25)   Not forsaking the assembly of ourselves together, as the manner of some is; But exhorting one another: And so much the more, as ye see the day approaching.

In none of these verses used by those with lucifer's system of thought to change times and laws, does it say that the apostles did not observe the commanded seventh day of rest anymore. In not one place in the whole bible does it say that the commanded Sabbath day of rest ever stopped being observed on the seventh day. Jesus himself actually says to not think that he came to change the law or to destroy the prophets or the need for prophets. Yet this system of lucifer's has those that falsely teach of a change and that prophets are not used or needed even in these days. Jesus said himself that he did not destroy the position or need of profits, only fulfilled the law of sacrifice setting us free for a time from man's greed and control. All these verses do is prove that the apostles were gathering like they were told to, and nowhere does it say or imply that they were told to gather on any specific day. No commandment or word from Jesus, the apostles or even God himself made the first day of the week a Sabbath day. Nor did theymark the first day as the only day to gather or to do the works commissioned by Jesus. I would challenge anyone to show where we were commanded to worship only one day a week and to only work on the great commission one day a week. We must also be careful not to forget the only requirement Jesus himself gives for the definition of a gathering, and is why no gathering defined as so can truly be denied and stopped. Refusing Jesus's definition is the only true way to stop all gatherings, and is what lucifer aims for with twisting and denying God's commands, making many puffed up thinking they are greater because of large numbers.

Matthew 18:20

20)   "For where two or three are gathered together in my name, there am I in the midst of them".

There is nothing wrong with gathering often. The issue arises when we assume that gathering means we do not have to obey God's commands anymore. When we allow lucifer to trick us into no longer observing something we were told, nay, commanded to remember and to keep holy for all generations until the end of time. We allow a system of thought fathered by lucifer and instilled in selfish men that act like kings to change times and laws, to teach others to do the same, with not one ounce of proof or evidence to justify it. Only a goal to undermine the authority of God the Father and take Jesus's role as head of the body and rob the saints of rest, wearing them out so they will be seen missing the mark at Jesus's return.

To really get down to the change of the seventh day of rest and who thought to change it and teach others to do so without question, we have to start with who first changed the days from numbers which are used in the bible from front to back, to names that represent false gods that the Romans worshiped. The Romans mainly worshiped the sun god, so naturally this growing system of thought that believed it could change times and laws, adopted the seven names we know as the days of the week. This is when this system of thought that was corrupting the Scribes and the Pharisees took the opportunity to erase God's commanded seventh day of rest, which will trick his people into working on a day that was set aside by God himself for rest and rejuvenation, making all that do spiritually dead for forgetting and defiling his commanded day of rest. Then with no biblical proof or justification, this Roman system moves the day of rest to the first day of the week, and successfully because again, the people did not have the scriptures to read for themselves, and by the time anyone did and asked about any discrepancies, were simply told either he wasn't serious when he said that or we are not holy and therefore could not know any better, even though Jesus tells us that it will be the Holy Ghost that reveals truth to us. They then call the new day Sun-day, after the sun god that this system originally worshiped, when God the Father says that the seventh day of rest will be a sign between him and his people for all generations until the end of time. Changing this day is like someone giving us directions to wait at a specific place, then an enemy that does not want us to arrive changes the meeting location, for no more reason than to confuse and cause problems. This is why we have the parable of the 10 virgins waiting for the bridegroom in Matthew 25:8,9. The enemy is always trying to steal our oil so we will not be prepared for when Jesus returns. The rejuvenation that the sabbath day of rest gives is the oil that keeps our lamps burning bright and is what lucifer is successfully stealing from so many.

    It was Roman Emperor Constantine I that was the first to issue a mass day of rest on the pagan day of sun-day in 321 A.D. This diverse system that lucifer infiltrated as he did with the Scribes and the Pharisees that could devour and manipulate kings, that can be identified by attempting to change times, laws and defy Jesus's smallest commands like calling no man father on earth, with no more of an argument than, "Oh, he wasn't serious when he said that"; This system that still piles on burdens to sell salvation made the official change of the commanded seventh day Sabbath of rest to the first day of the week, called Sun-day to represent the sun god, in 336 A.D. by the Roman Catholic church in the council of Laodicea. The Roman Church has admitted to and even documented the change and has no more excuse for it than the one they learned to do it from. Then teach others to do the same starting all others off on the wrong path to begin with. Many became too eager to separate from this system of thought that infiltrated like with the Scribes and Pharisees, that they did not slow down enough to see the heaviest of mistakes they carried on with. The sad part is we have the scriptures today that tell us the truth of these mistakes and too many ignore it for selfish reasons. Do we trust and obey God or not? Is America a God fearing country or not? The answers are in our fruits and our ability to obey God's commands. As of today with the baby sacrifices and helping in the defiling of his little ones and all other manner of evil breeding in this country, America is looking like the whore in Revelation as our Great statue of liberty promotes and stands for the protection for these evil deeds of Sodom and Gomorrah. If God the Father said that the observation of the seventh day of rest is a mark to show that we are his, wouldn't forgetting this day of rest and defiling it be a mark of lucifer or the beast? Many won't see the folly of this corrupted system until a blue law is put into action and we are in the same situation spoken of in the book of Daniel.

    I find it odd that so many will beat each other and judge one another harshly with single verses. So many claim to be of the bible yet will ignore so much evidence to keep from feeling wrong. Jesus said that he made it so simple that a child can understand it. I believe we make it complicated by running from and excusing the truth of our selfishness that breeds all of the deadly sins in our lives daily. My purpose is to make demons nervous and uncomfortable, not to attack the houses of prayer that belong to Christ Jesus, only to remind that even the religious leaders of Jesus's day, who sat in the seat of Moses, were influenced by lucifer's system of thought and had to be rebuked first in order to flip their magnets back around. And as Jesus made their demons nervous as he called them out, they lashed out at having their corruption and selfishness called out as they hid behind holy things. Our actions will always find us out eventually. Just as those influenced by the same system of thought will choose to attack me instead of actually searching what I say. Are we to believe that lucifer just left things alone after Jesus's death and resurrection? Jesus even told us the traits that those with this system would exhibit while under lucifer's selfish venom. We know, thanks to Jesus, how they will like to dress, where they like to sit, how they will act and speak in public and even what they will like to be called. Imagine that it just happens to be all the things Jesus commands us not to do. And when asked about it, one is given an answer that questions the seriousness of the most high like lucifer in the garden. Keep in mind that God the Father and Jesus drew out lucifer's system of thought by saying not to do something, knowing the nature and desires of lucifer.

    I believe that Jesus Christ is the only one to ever die on a cross in humanity's place to fulfill the law of sacrifice for all who would believe in him. I believe that the law reveals our selfish nature and shows us that we could try to pay with sacrifices for an eternity and it would still never be enough. This understanding helps us to see why we need a savior to bridge the gap caused by humanity's selfishness. Our submission to Jesus's system of thought, his example, slowly shapes and molds us one day at a time to be less selfish and more selfless. I believe Jesus did command us to gather often, to help lift each other out of this selfish crab bucket. I believe that no matter how often we gather to pray, for Jesus himself said his house is a house of prayer, we worship daily by doing as he commanded by being kind and forgiving to each other. It does not nullify the command to remember and honor the seventh day Sabbath of rest.

I have often thought about the words of Jesus in Matthew.

Matthew 7:22,23
22) "Many will say to me in that day, Lord, Lord, have we not prophesied in thy name? And in thy name have cast out devils? And in thy name done many wonderful works?
23) and then will I profess unto them, I never knew you: Depart from me, ye that work iniquity".

Matthew 5:18-20
18) "For verily I say unto you, till heaven and earth pass, one jot or one tittle shall in no wise pass from the law, till all be fulfilled.
19) Whosoever therefore shall break one of these least commandments, and teach men so, he shall be called the least in the kingdom of heaven: But whosoever shall do and teach them, the same shall be called great in the kingdom of heaven.
20) For I say unto you, that except your righteousness shall exceed the righteousness of the scribes and Pharisees, ye shall in no case enter the kingdom of heaven".

I often wondered if these people did these great things in the name of Jesus, how did they end up being rejected? Then I had to ask myself, because asking is part of seeking, did they remember and honor the day that marks us as his people for all generations? Did they remember and honor the day that was set aside and made holy by God the Father himself? Or did they believe the very same lie that lucifer tricked Eve with instead of reading for themselves? Never even asking why lucifer worked so hard to change the day, what Jesus said his house is to be called as well as what worship even is. Things of this nature I see like sighting in a gun. We can put a gun in a vice so that it cannot move at all. We can set a target at 100 feet and sight the gun in until it hits just off the center bullseye, but still in the bullseye circle. So many call it good simply because the bullseye is hit and become satisfied. Only, as the target is moved further away, the farther from the bullseye the shot gets, until the shot misses the target altogether. This is lucifer's plan, to change just enough laws and times to where the people still think the bullseye is being hit. Make them move so fast and focused on other things that we do not see or question the short sightedness, and when it is questioned, we are satisfied with an answer from lucifer. Only, after so much time has passed with each generation saying, "It's ok, it won't surely hurt anything," we will be seen missing the mark and will be rejected for it. All because we were too slothful to ask, seek and knock for ourselves because we were too busy chasing things of this world. I believe God's word when he said that he hallowed it and it would be a sign between him and his people for all time and generations.

    The Evidence for the case for the seventh day Sabbath is pretty one sided and overwhelmingly for the seventh day. There is actually not even one piece of evidence for anything else, yet many will still mock and dismiss this evidence because of fear and or pride. We will even see the heart of lucifer come out in some as their first response to these truths will be with the nature of lucifer, to lash out, argue and even insult and be violent instead of simply searching and praying about it, as seen with the Scribes and Pharisees. Lest we forget that it was the religious leaders with the authority of Moses that fell to lucifer's system of thought and had Jesus Christ killed. With all of this evidence for the commanded seventh day of rest, it amazes me that Christians eager to throw stones, forget to take the time to look in that mirror and pull out the beam in their own eye, as they are tricked into changing and forgetting not only what we were commanded to remember, but also how to enter into his rest and the benefits of obeying. Many forget that the message in 2 Timothy is for misled Christians also, not just for the lost sheep. But for all that refuse to believe and listen to undeniable truths, for fear of admitting that lucifer has fooled masses into forgetting what God himself said will mark us as his people.

2 Timothy 4:3,4

3) For the time will come when they will not endure sound doctrine; but after their own lusts shall they heap to themselves teachers, having itching ears;

4) And they shall turn away their ears from the truth, and shall be turned unto fables.

I only pray this inspires questions into what I believe to be a serious topic. Do not take my word for it though. Read and study, ask, seek and knock, search and pray for Jesus to increase our understanding by the Holy Ghost of his day of rest. I pray that we will see as we observe the seventh day Sabbath and enter into his rest, that we also see how the rejuvenation helps us to see the Holy Ghost's poetry in motion more clearly. I pray we begin to understand that learning to live one day at a time and observing his day of rest, is how we slow enough to hear that still small voice that is the Holy Ghost trying to work all things for good, including what was meant for evil. Finally, I pray we would learn and remember not only what day the proper sabbath day of rest is, but also that the rejuvenation gained from observing that day of rest, is what keeps our lamps full of oil so our lights will be burning bright when Jesus comes back, and that this is the very reason why lucifer works so hard to twist and pervert. May we learn that when God says not to do something, he is setting lucifer up to show himself and hang himself with his own rope, because lucifer will always show himself and his system of thought by doing exactly what God has said not to do and what Jesus says not to do. He will work hard to make us forget what we were told to remember and defile what he said to keep holy. May we remember to take the same advice we give others and make sure the same scriptures we use to throw stones do not convict us as well.

FOR THE PROFIT OF ALL

Through my experience and desires to know, for the Lord says those that seek shall find. I have come to realize that one of the masterkeys is learning to accept the shaping and molding process we take on when following in Christ's footsteps. We often ask for help then get mad when the help requires us to look at ourselves real good. Most times we do not like what we see. I believe this is why Jesus was adamant about not judging others unrighteously.

Matthew 7:7
7) "Ask, and it shall be given you; Seek, and ye shall find; Knock, and it shall be opened unto you:"

Matthew 7:1-5
1) "Judge not, that ye be not judged.
2) For with what judgment ye judge, ye shall be judged: and with what measure ye mete, it shall be measured to you again.
3) And why beholdest thou the mote that is in thy brother's eye, but considerest not the beam that is in thine own eye?
4) Or how wilt thou say to thy brother, let me pull out the mote out of thine eye; and, behold, a beam is in thine own eye?
5) Thou hypocrite, first cast out the beam out of thine own eye; And then shalt thou see clearly to cast out the mote out of thy brother's eye".

We are held up to the very same standards that we place on others. If we do not like liars and judge them harshly; We better not be guilty of lying at all because Jesus will point it out. If we do not like adulterers; We better not be committing adultery, and remember, Jesus himself said that thinking it is the same as doing it in his eyes and he will be the judge. If we do not like people talking about us and taking advantage of us; We better not take advantage of others or talk about them behind their backs. Jesus calls for us to take an inward look at ourselves before we ever evaluate others. That inward look is what turned the ones away that were wanting to cast stones at Mary.

John 8:7-9

7) So when they continued asking him, he lifted up himself, and said unto them, "He that is without sin among you, let him cast a stone at her".
8) And again he stooped down, and wrote on the ground.
9) And they which heard it, being convicted by their own conscience, went out one by one, beginning at the eldest, even unto the last: And Jesus was left alone, and the woman standing in the midst.

The lack of an inward look is what makes it easier for many to ignore what we see in ourselves, only to focus on what we see in others. Looking inward first is part of the shaping and molding process. It is actually kind of the start. We often remember that we are told to come as we are, especially when we want others to accept the selfishness we carry with us. We forget that this does not mean we get to stay the way we are. Coming as we are is Jesus's way of saying that we do not have to change to start the process of change, only come and start as we are. Those that teach that we have to change and be right before coming to Jesus are doing a disservice to the great commission and the works of the Holy Ghost. Jesus offers forgiveness as well as the examples and lessons to follow that change our selfish nature that causes all of our problems, to a selfless nature that is able to endure all problems. This is what Jesus means when he says we have to be born again. Although we do not have to change to approach Jesus, we do have to be born again in order to enter his kingdom.

Isaiah 1:18

18) Come now, and let us reason together, saith the Lord: Though your sins be as scarlet, they shall be as snow; Though they be red like crimson, they shall be as wool.

Matthew 11:28

28) "Come unto me, all ye that labour and are heavy laden, and I will give you rest".

1 Corinthians 6:9-11

9) Know ye not that the unrighteous shall not inherit the kingdom of God? Be not deceived: Neither fornicators, nor idolaters, nor adulterers, nor effeminate, nor abusers of themselves with mankind,

10) Nor thieves, nor covetous, nor drunkards, nor revilers, nor extortioners, shall inherit the kingdom of God.

11) And such were some of you: But ye are washed, but ye are sanctified, but ye are justified in the name of the Lord Jesus, and by the spirit of our God.

2 Corinthians 5:17,18

17) Therefore if any man be in Christ, he is a new creature: Old things are passed away; Behold, all things are become new.

18) And all things are of God, who hath reconciled us to himself by Jesus Christ, and hath given to us the ministry of reconciliation.

Galatians 2:20

20) I am crucified with Christ: Nevertheless I live; Yet not I, but Christ liveth in me: And the life which I now live in the flesh by the faith of the son of God, who loved me, gave himself for me.

Revelation 22:17

17) And the spirit and the bride say, come. And let him that heareth say, come. And let him that is athirst come. And whosoever will, let him take the water of life freely.

The shaping and molding process we go through on our walk with Christ is a lifelong process of him adding and taking away. When we accept Jesus and start his process of change, his spirit is what is within us cleaning house as we walk with him. Our selfish attachments to the sins that are destroying our world makes it harder for the potter to shape the clay. The change does not happen overnight and even the apostles stumbled and got up many times on their walk with Jesus. Many of us have many layers to pull back. Understanding this helps us to realize that we all are going through the same process of being shaped and molded. Many of us make it more like blacksmithing with our stubbornness. Many get scared of the change required and fall back into ignorance and unbelief, refusing to look inward and throwing stones at anyone that makes us see our own selfishness. We let this selfish attachment to sin and its illusionary pleasures make us ignore the words that plainly say that we cannot enter heaven the way we are. We have to be vaccinated from the virus of selfishness.

    Some on the other hand, continue to go through the lifelong shaping and molding process enduring to the end, proving to God the Father that we are serious about choosing him over our own selfishness. Through this process we gain empathy and understanding for others and their struggles. Because of this, we become better helpers to others. We often forget that while we are each undergoing change in one direction or another, we cannot force others to change just as others cannot force us to change. We can help others in their struggles just as others can help us in ours, but they cannot carry our burdens just as we cannot carry theirs. Our help for one another has to come from a heart of understanding, which always seems to go back to that inward look first. It becomes apparent that it is our experiences that Jesus helps us with that we share with each other, so that not only are we always reminded that Jesus works in our lives daily, but that so many others go through the same struggles and need help as well. We never know when sharing how Jesus helped us overcome our selfish sin will encourage someone else to call on and rely on Jesus for help.

The process begins to reveal the intent to chip away the selfish parts of us. The process is designed to change our thoughts and habits from a "Me" thought process to a "We". Jesus's whole ministry was to fulfill the law of sacrifice, to teach us and to show us that we are all sinners ruled by our selfish desires going through the same storms, and that he is the only way through the storms that our selfishness causes. We are all guilty of a crime that required the sacrifice of a willing sinless man. Since we are all in the same boat that is sailing to hell, we are called to show the same mercy, love and forgiveness to others that we want from our Father in heaven. This is why Jesus tells a parable about this very issue. Notice that it is one of the many parables that Jesus says that heaven is like. We should always pay close attention when he is trying to tell us what heaven is like or what the judgment process will be like. He is after all our judge and high priest.

Matthew 18:21-35

21) Then came Peter to him, and said, Lord, how oft shall my brother sin against me, and I forgive him? Till seven times?
22) Jesus saith unto him, "I say not unto thee, until seven times: But seventy times seven.
23) Therefore is the kingdom of heaven likened unto a certain king, which would take account of his servants.
24) And when he had begun to reckon, one was brought unto him, which owed him ten thousand talents.
25) But for as much as he had not to pay, his Lord commanded him to be sold, and his wife, and children, and all that he had, and payment to be made.
26) The servant therefore fell down, and worshiped him, saying, Lord, have patience with me, and I will pay thee all.
27) Then the Lord of that servant was moved with compassion, and loosed him, and forgave him the debt.
28) But the same servant went out, and found one of his fellow servants, which owed him an hundred pence: And he laid hands on him, and took him by the throat, saying, pay me that thou owest.

29) And his fellow servant fell down at his feet, and besought him, saying, have patience with me, and I will pay thee all.
30) And he would not: But went and cast him into prison, till he should pay the debt.
31) So when his fellow servants saw what was done, they were very sorry, and came and told unto their Lord all that was done.
32) Then his Lord, after that he had called him, said unto him, o thou wicked servant, I forgave thee all that debt, because thou desiredst me:
33) Shouldest not thou also have had compassion on thy fellow servant, even as I had pity on thee?
34) And his Lord was wroth, and delivered him to the tormentors, till he should pay all that was due unto him.
35) So likewise shall my Heavenly Father do also unto you, if ye from your hearts forgive not every one his brother their trespasses".

Matthew 6:12

12) "And forgive us our debts as we forgive our debtors".

Matthew 21:33-40

33) "Hear another parable: There was a certain householder, which planted a vineyard, and hedged it round about, and digged a winepress in it, and built a tower, and let it out to husbandmen, and went into a far country:
34) And when the time of the fruit drew near, he sent his servants to the husbandmen, that they might receive the fruits of it.
35) And the husbandmen took his servants, and beat one, and killed another, and stoned another.
36) Again, he sent other servants more than the first: And they did unto them likewise.
37) But last of all he sent unto them his son, saying, they will reverence my son.

38)   But when the husbandmen saw the son, they said among themselves, this is the heir: Come, let us kill him, and let us seize on his inheritance.
39)   And they caught him, and cast him out of the vineyard, and slew him.
40)   When the Lord therefore of the vineyard cometh, what will he do unto those husbandmen"?

This parable teaches that the servants were the prophets, the son is Jesus and the Lord of the vineyard is God the Father. The husbandmen are the ones God made stewards over his vineyard, his church which is a people, not a building made with human hands. The husbandmen become infected by selfishness and intend to rob the son of his inheritance. In this story, we catch a glimpse of the story of the Scribes, Pharisees and the system of thought that is lucifers along with all that fall into his traps and follow the mistakes of the Pharisees, that seeks the power and authority of the most high. Many of Jesus's parables give glimpses of why we are here and what we are supposed to do, or at least what is expected of us. But our selfishness blinds us to his warnings, and therefore allows lucifer to pluck his seeds of wisdom from our understanding like a bird robbing seeds from the sower.
    While we are not called to judge, we are called to evaluate. Which is what we need to learn to do so that we can identify truth and false, wicked and non wicked. Many do not see a difference, but how does a physician know what ailment to treat if he does not evaluate the patient first? How does Judge or jury make a judgment without evaluating the case first? Many forget that it is possible to evaluate without judging, just as we can judge without first evaluating. Jesus does not say to not point out the sin of others, only to look inward first and make sure we are not guilty of the same sin. Jesus says to remove the beam from our own eye first, so we may see more clearly to remove the mote from our brother's eye. I find it funny how he uses the size difference, implying possibly that usually if we look inward first, the bigger sin is most times in us. We also must

be sure that our reason for pointing out sin is not rooted in selfishness. Are we pointing it out due to our own envy, greed, lust, pride or so on? If so, it is for selfish reasons and not out of love and correction. We are to weigh our thoughts and actions against this balance scale daily. I believe we are to show mercy and understanding when revealing personal sins to others. Not to embarrass or make anyone less, and certainly not to feed our own selfish egos. We are told not to cast our pearls before swine. How do we know what dogs and swine are without an evaluation first? We are taught the way to evaluate each other is through our actions. Not words mostly, but our actions and how much we love.

Matthew 7:16-20

16) "Ye shall know them by their fruits. Do men gather grapes of thorns, or figs of thistles?
17) even so every good tree bringeth forth good fruit; But a corrupt tree bringeth forth evil fruit.
18) A good tree cannot bring forth evil fruit, neither can a corrupt tree bring forth good fruit.
19) Every tree that bringeth not forth good fruit is hewn down, and cast into the fire.
20) Wherefore by their fruits ye shall know them".

We are taught as kids that actions are louder than words. So we are to evaluate each other based on how we treat each other, and not just those we like. How we treat our enemies and those we see as lesser than ourselves says a lot about our character as well.

Luke 6:32-35

32) "For if ye love them which love you, what thank have ye? For even sinners also love those that love them.
33) And if ye do good to them which do good to you, what thank have ye? For sinners also do even the same.
34) And if ye lend to them of whom ye hope to receive, what thank have ye? For sinners also lend to sinners, to receive as much again.

35)   But love ye your enemies, and do good, and lend, hoping for nothing again; And your reward shall be great, and ye shall be the children of the highest: For he is kind unto the unthankful and to the evil.

We are supposed to treat each other like we ourselves want to be treated. It all sounds pretty simple. We messed up, we are put in time out on a planet that is exactly like everything else in our existence, it starts dying as soon as it is born. In a way, it is like an hourglass counting down to the end. So this planet will eventually die and blow up, get hit by an asteroid or comet and blow up or humanity will blow it up through its selfishness. We have a chance to go home and be forgiven but someone has to come bridge the gap and pay for the selfishness of humanity and all of the evil that it created. Someone has to come and teach us how to go home. Someone has to open our eyes to the truth and be the way to show us the life we are to be found living when Jesus comes the second time. Instead of a mythical hero, he was one who tried to teach us the rules of judgment. That learning to forgive, love and show mercy to others is key to the forgiveness we need to be accepted home. He was simplifying what lucifer spent so long trying to complicate within the leadership of not just past religious institutions, but all that followed that would fall into the same traps that the Scribes and Pharisees did.
Some think salvation is in only one or the other, in faith or in works. I tell you it is in both together, not apart.

James 2:17-26

17)   Even so faith, if it hath not works, is dead, being alone.
18)   Yea, a man may say, thou hast faith, and I have works: Shew me thy faith without thy works, and I will shew thee my faith by my works.
19)   Thou believest that there is one God; Thou doest well: The devils also believe, and tremble.
20)   But wilt thou know, o vain man, that faith without works is dead?

21) Was not Abraham our father justified by works, when he had offered Issac his son upon the altar?
22) Seest thou how faith wrought with his works, and by works was faith made perfect?
23) And the scripture was fulfilled which saith, Abraham believed God, and it was imputed unto him for righteousness: and he was called the friend of God.
24) Ye see then how that by works a man is justified, and not by faith only.
25) Likewise also was not Rahab the harlot justified by works, when she had received the messenger, and had sent them out another way?
26) For as the body without the spirit is dead, so faith without works is dead also.

     Faith is nothing without works just as works are nothing without faith. We are all falling and our works are the measure of our reach to Jesus, just as our faith is the measure of Jesus's reach to us. Only with both is the grip made and salvation complete. Many misunderstand this lesson due to a fear or refusal to change, or simply out of spiritual slothfulness. Yes, faith is the most important because it is true faith and understanding of our forgiveness that lights the fire in us to work. If we say we have faith but do not have works, we do not fully understand all we were forgiven for. If we truly believe Jesus and not just in him, we know that we all were commissioned to go to work. A true walk with Jesus builds a desire to do the work of Christ, hence we will know them by their fruits and/or works. Take the story of the woman and the perfume for example.

Luke 7:37-50

37) And, behold, a woman in the city, which was a sinner, when she knew that Jesus sat at meat in the Pharisees' house , brought an alabaster box of ointment,
38) And stood at his feet behind him weeping, and began to wash his feet with tears, and did wipe them with the hairs of her

head, and kissed his feet, and anointed them with the ointment.
39)   Now when the Pharisee which had bidden him saw it, he spake within himself, saying, this man, if he were a prophet, would have known who and what manner of woman this is that toucheth him: For she is a sinner.
40)   And Jesus answering said unto him, "Simon, I have somewhat to say unto thee". And he saith, master, say on.
41)   "There was a certain creditor which had two debtors: The one owed five hundred pence, and the other fifty.
42)   And when they had nothing to pay, he frankly forgave them both. Tell me therefore, which of them will love him most"?
43)   Simon answered and said, I suppose that he, to whom he forgave most. And he said unto him, "thou hast rightly judged".
44)   And he turned to the woman, and said unto Simon, "seest thou this woman? I entered into thine house, thou gavest me no water for my feet: But she hath washed my feet with tears, and wiped them with the hairs of her head.
45)   Thou gavest me no kiss: But this woman since the time I came in hath not ceased to kiss my feet.
46)   My head with oil thou didst not anoint: But this woman hath anointed my feet with ointment.
47)   Wherefore I say unto thee, her sins, which are many, are forgiven; For she loved much: But to whom little is forgiven, the same loveth little".
48)   And he said unto her, "Thy sins are forgiven".
49)   And they that sat at meat with him began to say within themselves, who is this that forgiveth sins also?
50)   And he said to the woman, "Thy faith hath saved thee; Go in peace".

Not only does Jesus let us know that we can tell a person's fruits by the love they show, or do not show, and that we can gauge where we stand in forgiveness by the amount we love, but also that works is a part of our faith. For though he told her that her faith saved her, it was her show of love and the works of that love that truly showed her faith. Her faith would never have been shown without her works which showed any looking, that she understood the depth of all she was forgiven. Works go hand in hand with true faith because faith brings a desire to follow Christ, and truly following Christ produces a desire to share the salvation he offers, which requires work, simple as that. Lukewarm believers spend a life refusing works as a form of spiritual laziness. They tell the world that they have faith, but just not enough to do any work that benefits the work of the great commission. They say they love their neighbors yet do not even care to share the news of Jesus that they themselves benefit from. If we truly are believers yet do not work towards the great commission, are we not then letting our laziness make us watch our brothers and sisters burn? Salvation through faith alone is reserved for those that come to Christ late in their life or before the age of accountability, like the thief on the cross, although even the thief showed a bit of love and works by defending Jesus from the other thief's mockery. If we claim to be a follower or believer in Christ our whole life, yet have no works, what is the proof of our claimed faith? What is the proof of our love for the body of Christ? Because it does not matter when we come to Christ and go to work, Just that we go to work and in the end, we all receive the same pay, forgiveness. This lesson is taught in a parable Jesus told, and needs to be learned by lifelong Christians that believe they are better than those new to the faith. Again, he starts with what heaven is like.

Matthew 20:1-16

1) " For the kingdom of heaven is like unto a man that is an householder, which went out early in the morning to hire laborers into his vineyard.

2) And when he had agreed with the laborers for a penny a day, he sent them into his vineyard.

3) And he went out about the third hour, and saw others standing idle in the marketplace,

4) And said unto them; Go ye also into the vineyard, and whatsoever is right I will give you. And they went their way.

5) Again he went out about the sixth and ninth hour, and did likewise.
6) And about the eleventh hour he went out, and found others standing idle, and saith unto them, why stand ye here all the day idle?
7) They say unto him, because no man hath hired us. He saith unto them, go ye also into the vineyard; And whatsoever is right, that shall ye receive.
8) So when even was come, the Lord of the vineyard saith unto his steward, call the laborers, and give them their hire, beginning from the last unto the first.
9) And when they came that were hired about the eleventh hour, they received every man a penny.
10) But when the first came, they supposed that they should have received more; And they likewise received every man a penny.
11) And when they received it, they murmured against the goodman of the house.
12) Saying, these last have wrought but one hour, and thou hast made them equal unto us, which have borne the burden and heat of the day.
13) But he answered one of them, and said, friend, I do thee no wrong: Didst not thou agree with me for a penny?
14) Take that thine is, and go thy way: I will give unto this last, even as unto thee.
15) Is it not lawful for me to do what I will with mine own? Is thine eye evil, because I am good?
16) So the last shall be first, and the first last: For many be called, but few chosen".

We all need to remember that God the Father is the great planner and orchestrator of all things good. Only he knows when and how to call his laborers to work because only he knows how hot our fires can burn and for how long. So we need to work when our faith calls us to quit being idle, only depending on our faith alone, and not let our selfish pride and envy think we are more than a laborer called in the late hours of the harvest.

We are to keep in mind daily the struggle to battle selfishness, which is the mother of all sins that plague the world that we were to tend. It is a daily fight, that we are to ask help with on a daily basis

Luke 11:3

3) "Give us day by day our daily bread".

He did not say to give us this week or this month, he said day by day. We do most of our stumbling and falling when we forget our savior and we extend ourselves beyond one day at a time with our selfish desires. Slowing down enough to see it is the key to seeing the poetry in motion that is the spirit of God trying to work all things for good. Slowing down with true intent is how we start to hear that still small voice. Lucifer knows this as well. This is why he works hard to make humanity move faster and faster, keeping so many chasing selfish things that we do not even notice the snakes eating eggs in the hen house. Luckily there is hope in the belief in Jesus. At times it can be hard, but we are assured that all things are possible through Jesus.

Philippians 4:13

13) I can do all things through Christ which strengthens me.

We also need to understand that part of that belief in him means believing and doing what he says. If we believe what he says, then we do what he says. We often forget that his recipe for a stress free life hinged on living a sinless and selfless life. Since we will never be perfect, how stress free we live is based on how hard we try to overcome our own selfishness. Putting down those chains of desire that cause much of the stress in our lives. Selfishness is born into us as well as taught and learned. Jesus's system of thought pushes back the selfish nature allowing us to see what life could be like without it. But as the population grows and the balance between believers and non believers continues to change, the world suffers and the results of our selfishness touch all believers and non believers, slowly corrupting the tree and its fruit. All because we as followers of Christ do not have the sternness of his people of old. We sometimes let lucifer trick us into believing that we are supposed to be around the truly selfish and/or wicked. Yes, Jesus hung out with sinners because he did not come for the righteous. He came looking for the ones, not the ninety nines. First, we are all sinners, every one of us from the prostitute on the street corner to the Pope. We are all guilty of some form of selfishness that we have to fight daily. Second, there are none that are righteous, only those that think they are.

Romans 3:9,10

9) What then? Are we better than they? No, in no wise: For we have before proved both Jews and Gentiles, that they are all under sin;
10) As it is written, there is none righteous, no, not one:

What everyone is not, is wicked. What Jesus did not hang out with, are those that are wicked and do wicked things. We often allow lucifer and his system of thought to make us forget there is a difference between the sinner which we all are, and the wicked which we all are not. We must remember this and know that we are not called to accept wickedness or be forced to associate with wicked people. Simple sinners that fight against their sin daily, yes; Wicked people that revel in and enjoy not only their sin, but eagerly corrupt future generations in order to please their own lack of self, no. We are called to forgive the wicked and do good to them, but we are not called to be a part of them and their deeds. We let ridiculous excuses chain us to people, places and situations. We allow lucifer to make us forget that there is a huge difference between those that are born again, which make up the body of Christ; And those that refuse to be born again, which are not a part of the body of Christ. I tend to look at it from my oilfield experience. On the surface, many standing outside looking in see the money that roughnecks make working on drilling rigs. They see the wives getting to run around and do all kinds of things. They see the things that they are able to buy or more accurately, the debt that they are able to take on. Others see all of this and want it for themselves, until they try to do the work and realize how much energy we have to put out daily and how much family time we give up in order to achieve what everyone sees. Many want the benefits but never want to do the work others put in to get it. Most last a day or two, before we never see them again. The lazy never last long in the oilfield. Christianity is the same. Many look from the outside and see things they want, but are never willing to do the work it takes to get it or keep it.

    Jesus unlocked the chains of selfishness that makes us envious, greedy, lustful and so on with his sacrifice. His life example showed us a different way to be, think and live. A different way to treat each other. What heaven on earth could look like. This is why he was careful about what he did and said. He knew that his words and actions would be talked about until the end of time as we know it. Jesus was teaching us not to be selfish and to think of others as equals, just a different part to a body, all working together for one goal. This is the lesson behind a body and its parts.

1 Corinthians 12:12-20

12)   For as the body is one, and hath many members, and all the members of that one body, being many, are one body: So also is Christ.

13)   For by one spirit are we all baptized into one body, whether we be Jews or Gentiles, whether we be bond or free; And have been all made to drink into one spirit.

14)   For the body is not one member, but many.

15)   If the foot shall say, because I am not the hand, I am not of the body; Is it therefore not of the body?

16)   And if the ear shall say, because I am not the eye, I am not of the body; Is it therefore not of the body?

17)   If the whole body were an eye, where were the hearing? If the whole body were the hearing, where were the smelling?

18)   But now hath God set the members every one of them in the body, as it hath pleased him.

19) And if they were all one member, where were the body?
20) But now are they many members, yet one body.

Many of us forget that these instructions are not only for the early church of Jesus's day, but for every believer and denomination of our time as well. We can see the need for this lesson as we see so many different denominations throwing stones at one another, fighting over who the head of the body is or who has the better spiritual gift, which is all that really separates many denominations and/or body parts. We have hands fighting over a foot's job and knees thinking they are better than the elbows. Each part fights so much that they neglect their gift or job, making the body dysfunctional. The fighting over whose gift is greatest makes the body of Christ fumble at the job it has on this earth, which is to fulfill the great commission given by Jesus himself. The only thing that can give any relief on learning this is that, even the apostles got caught by Jesus arguing over who the greatest among them was.

Luke 9:46
46) Then there arose a reasoning among them, which of them should be greatest.

Mark 9:33-36
33) And he came to Capernaum: And being in the house he asked them, "What was it that ye disputed among yourselves by the way"?
34) But they held their peace: For by the way they had disputed among themselves, who should be the greatest.
35) And he sat down, and called the twelve, and saith unto them, "If any man desire to be first, the same shall be last of all, and servant of all".

Many denominations forget what it means to be baptized into one body, the body of Christ. We can see this in how a person has to be re-baptized if we were to change denominations simply because our gift did not fit in there, and usually because each denomination covets there on spiritual gift but mocks and denies the others that the scriptures they claim to follow plainly point out. Baptism has become like a regulated initiation into a club with tithing tied to a person's worthiness, instead of the whole body of Christ that has many body parts, each with a gift and purpose, to aid each other in the work the body is to do. Each denomination was formed around one of the gifts of the spirit. They then build walls around that particular gift and throw stones at each other's gift, all proclaiming that they are the one and true. They shun even those among themselves that might have been born with a different gift than the denomination they were raised in. This is why one born with the gift of faith may not fit in with those that have the gift of tongues, even though this is only made possible because we allowed lucifer's system of thought to infiltrate and trick us into thinking we are greatest, so we throw stones and make fun of others even in front of other believers. Thinking that one's own gift is the greatest does not make one gift better than another. Being different only means we are a different body part of the same body with a different purpose and this is ok. This is the lesson behind using magnets to represent the spirit that holds the body of Christ together. Too many parts have their magnets backwards and need to get them flipped around so the whole body can come together. This can only happen if each body part stops fighting over Jesus' spot, the head, and all work for the profit and success for all. Lucifer's system of thought has infiltrated just as he did with the Scribes and Pharisees, to the point that they no longer see each other as body parts to a whole, and in doing so, have become too prideful and arrogant to understand how the Apostle Paul's lesson is just as needed these days as it was then.

1 Corinthians 12:3-11
3) Wherefore I give you to understand, that no man speaking by the spirit of God calleth Jesus accursed: and that no man can say that Jesus is the Lord, but by the Holy Ghost.
4) Now there are diversities of gifts, but the same spirit.
5) And there are differences of administrations, but the same Lord.

6) And there are diversities of operation, but it is the same God which worketh all in all.
7) But the manifestation of the spirit is given to every man to profit withal.
8) For to one is given by the spirit the word of wisdom; To another the word of knowledge by the same spirit;
9) To another faith by the same spirit; To another the gift of healing by the same spirit;
10) To another the working of miracles; To another prophecy; To another discerning of spirits; To another divers kinds of tongues; To another the interpretation of tongues:
11) But all these worketh that one and the selfsame spirit, dividing to every man severally as he will.

Lucifer also knows that there are diversities of gifts that are given by the very spirit that testifies of Jesus Christ. He also knows that there are differences between denominations that are supposed to be serving the same Lord, Jesus Christ our Lord and Savior. Lucifer knows that there are diversities of ministries, all working in and through God the Father for the profit of all. This is why lucifer works so hard to divide, by getting each member of the body to fight over the one position that belongs to Jesus alone. This battle makes each body part think they are more than they are. In turn, they start seeing others and the gift that the spirit gave them as lesser, until we are so busy throwing stones that we cannot fulfill the great commission as Jesus wanted. It is sad to think that the ones with the gift of discerning tongues, might be throwing stones at who they are supposed to work with. The real question is, If the different body parts got their magnets turned around right, what would we become that has lucifer so set on keeping everyone divided?

Denominations are not the only place that this same lesson applies. We also see a need for Jesus's system of thought as we look at the struggles in marriages, friendships, businesses, organizations, governments and even whole cultures themselves. Each one of these can be seen as a body that has many different parts, all designed differently to accomplish a common goal or purpose. Our selfishness makes the body work improper because it is always in chaos. Always busy throwing stones at each other thinking that the gifts and talents they possess are better and more important than others. When the body parts of any body, again, this logic applies to more than just religion. When they become more concerned about the profit of self over the profit of all, the body no longer works at one hundred percent and begins to slowly fall apart. We see this in families and businesses all of the time, only we never seem to blame it on what really caused the problems, selfishness. Selfishness teaches that the top is the only place to be and all under the head is lesser. Being Christlike or selfless, teaches that there is no body without the parts. Many would point out those with missing limbs just to appease the argumentative spirit they carry around. No one is ever happy to lose a body part. A body does not always go back to one hundred percent after a loss and it puts a strain on the other parts to even try. It takes all parts working together equally for any body to work at its best. Each part serves and thinks about the others, making no one part more important than another. A body truly working together means that everything we say and do should be for the profit of all, not just our own family and friends, for we are all brothers and sisters in Christ, and not just for select groups or certain organizations, but for all of humanity as a whole, as a body.

    To stay in this frame of mind, we have to learn the lesson from the Lord's prayer, taking things day by day, one day at a time. It becomes easy to trip over the things of today because we become too focused on tomorrow or yesterday. We give the Father thanks and recognition daily as we ask him for our daily bread. This daily recognition helps us to remember that we are all a body part that is gifted to benefit the whole body. We remember that it is ok to be the part that we are, with the gifts we are gifted with, and that we are at our best when we are working for the profit of all. We see in today's society the chaos and inferiority it causes, when all of society is bombarded with the gifts and talents of others. Envy is using social media to destroy our youth and their mental health. Then we wonder why our youth have so many emotional battles that they should not even have to deal with yet.

    Over time, I believe we finally understand that in overcoming our own selfishness, we figure out how to battle sin within ourselves, and within any body that has many parts. All sin; Envy, Gluttony, Greed, Lust, Pride, Sloth and Wrath; Are products of selfishness. Therefore all problems that plague families, friends, denominations, businesses, governments and even cultures, are derived from selfishness. Pride is the easiest to see as we parade all kinds of pride. Culture pride, country pride, state pride, city pride, school pride, family pride, work pride and there are plenty more in between. Selfish pride always comes before a fall and is why we have to become born again, and we are not born again until we see the need for a cure to this selfishness we were all born with. How do we fight or react to our own selfishness? By practicing selflessness. We sometimes forget that Jesus did not tell Mary to go and not get caught again. He did not even tell her to simply try harder next time. He told Mary to go and sin no more. Implying that this should be our goal, not simply learning to live with it. Enduring to the end means fighting against our selfish nature to the end, not living with it till the end. We flee from external temptations and fight the selfishness within ourselves by practicing selflessness. Jesus had a reason for teaching us to be kind and giving without seeking praise.

John 8:11

11) She said, no man, Lord. And Jesus said unto her, "Neither do I condemn thee: Go, and sin no more".

Matthew 5:43-48

43) "Ye have heard that it hath been said, thou shalt love thy neighbor, and hate thine enemy.
44) But I say unto you, love your enemies, bless them that curse you, do good to them that hate you, and pray for them which
despitefully use you, and persecute you:

45) That ye may be the children of your Father which is in heaven: For he maketh his sun to rise on the evil and on the good, and sendeth rain on the just and on the unjust.
46) For if ye love them which love you, what reward have ye? Do not even the publicans the same?
47) And if ye salute your brethren only, what do ye more than others? Do not even the publicans so?
48) Be ye therefore perfect, even as your Father which is in heaven is perfect".

We are encouraged to strive for perfection enduring to the end fighting against our own selfish desires. Choosing to be selfless because it makes the enemy flee and profits the whole body.

Matthew 6:1-4

1) "Take heed that ye do not your alms before men, to be seen of them: Otherwise ye have no reward of your Father which is in heaven.
2) Therefore when thou doest thine alms, do not sound a trumpet before thee, as hypocrites do in the synagogues and in the streets, that they may have glory of men. Verily I say unto you, They have their reward.
3) But when thou doest alms, let not thy left hand know what thy right hand doeth:
4) That thine alms may be in secret: And thy Father which seeth in secret himself shall reward thee openly".

James 4:7

7) submit yourselves therefore to God. Resist the devil, and he will flee from you.

Jesus in many ways, taught that he saw things differently than we do. He alone could see the intent in a person's heart, the sincerity in each person's circumstance. There is a reason why Jesus pointed out how a lowly woman putting in two mites was more than what anyone else had put in. Jesus looks at percent ages. He looks at the whole equation, not leaving parts out to make an illusionary answer that pushes a wicked agenda.

Mark 12:41-44

41) And Jesus sat over against the treasury, and beheld how the people cast money into the treasury: And many that were rich cast in much.
42) And there came a certain poor widow, and she threw in two mites, which make a farthing.
43) And he called unto him his disciples, and saith unto them, "Verily I say unto you, That this poor widow hath cast more in, than all they which have cast into the treasury:
44) For all they did cast in of their abundance; But she of her want did cast in all that she had, even all her living".

Jesus was pointing out that even though the rich seemed to be putting in a lot in comparison to the poor widow, Jesus saw that the rich put in about ten percent while the widow put in one hundred percent. The amount did not matter to Jesus, the sacrifice did. While many seem to pay the same, not all sacrifice the same and only Jesus sees the true measurement. Jesus was teaching that we are judged by our true intentions that only he sees, not by what we appear to intend. The sins that selfishness produces make us do things for ridiculous reasons. Many times we let these sins take us so far down a road that we feel like we can't go back. Jesus was trying to teach us that if each one of us would put the needs of others above our own selfish desires, everyone's needs would be met in the end with an abundance we could not imagine. Over time, people would have to do less and less as everyone thinks of others first and we become satisfied with our needs more than our selfish wants. These acts of selflessness not only battle against the selfishness that plagues humanity, but also gives us a glimpse of heaven on earth. Jesus taught us many ways of what heaven is like. He taught on how our forgiveness of others is tied to how we will be judged, that we will be measured by the very same ruler we use to measure others.

Matthew 7:1,2

1) "Judge not, that ye be not judged.
2) For with what judgment ye judge, ye shall be judged: And with what measure ye mete, it shall be measured to you again".

    We have to remember that this does not mean that we are to accept evil deeds. We are commanded to treat others like we ourselves want to be treated. We sometimes forget to ask if we would want others to let us get away with lying, stealing or murdering. Would we want society to really let us get away with defiling God's innocent ones? Jesus never says that we are not to point out the selfishness of others and the sins it breeds in our lives. We are actually instructed not only to do so, but how to by making sure we ourselves are innocent first. Which means we ourselves might have to go through the process of shedding a particular sin also. After we have removed our own sin, we can see clearly through our own experience to help our fellow brothers, and out of love and love only.

    In the end, if we learn to forgive and learn the lessons of what heaven is like through the stories, actions and events of Jesus, we would find ourselves making it home. We cannot have a selfish frame of mind in the kingdom of heaven. Our system of thought has to be reshaped from an all for one mentality to a mentality of one for all. When humanity reaches a point where the majority of its decisions are done for the profit of all; When we make sure that the things we think, say, and do are not influenced by Lust, Greed, Envy, Pride, or any of the sins that are mothered by selfishness; When our perspective of what is considered important is changedto each other, we will truly start to see heaven on earth and the poetry in motion that is the Holy Ghost guiding everyone to this realization.

    Too many of us, out of our fear of losing our material things, lash out at a system that teaches to think for the profit of all. Somehow lucifer tricks us into believing that this means we do not get to have anything, instead of understanding that this is Jesus's lesson to everyone about how to raise everyone up together. Many of us fight against it even though this is what Jesus is teaching us from God the Father. The simplest way I can think to explain this is with shopping carts. As we go shopping, we see many people too lazy, due to selfishness, to take their cart back to a cart holder. This laziness makes the job of the cart collector harder as he has to chase down stray carts. We see a mess many times with baskets left everywhere. This is how our world gets so messy due to the same selfishness. "If" each person thought for the profit of others and simply took a stray back to the cart holder with ours, or used a stray to shop with, there would eventually be no more stray baskets and the problem would slowly go away, and the job of the cart collector becomes easier, all because everyone put their selfishness aside. It is not about taking things from people, but getting people to understand how this system of thought, taught by Jesus, makes things easier for all in the long run and lifts us all up together. Yet our selfishness leaves the sick, poor and the needy at the bottom of this selfish crab bucket, as we race to get all we can like a mob on Black Friday. Again, this is an "if" scenario and points out the problem when a majority no longer carry the morals and values to not only think for the profit of all, but see the thought itself as an attack on our selfishness.

 I pray that the whole of humanity would slow down on its own to see this poetry in motion that encourages us all to work for the profit of all, before humanity is forced to slow down and it is too late to make a choice. I pray that in the end, the Lord will see humanity moving back to a majority that strive for the profit of all, as well as understanding that this system of thought that Jesus teaches is the only way back to the Father. Finally, I pray that we would see that Jesus' system of thought is the only reset to reverse and heal the damage caused by lucifer's system of thought.

SEEDS BY THE WAYSIDE

Matthew 13:1-23

1) The same day went Jesus out of the house, and sat by the sea side.
2) And great multitudes were gathered together unto him, so that he went into a ship, and sat; And the whole multitude stood on the shore.
3) And he spake many things unto them in parables, saying "Behold, a sower went forth to sow;
4) And when he sowed, some seeds fell by the way side, and the fowels came and devoured them up:
5) Some fell upon stony places, where they had not much earth: And forthwith they sprung up, because they had no deepness of earth:
6) And when the sun was up, they were scorched; And because they had no root, they withered away.
7) And some fell among thorns; And the thorns sprung up, and choked them:
8) But other fell into good ground, and brought forth fruit, some an hundredfold, some sixty, some thirtyfold.
9) Who hath ears to hear, let him hear".
10) And the disciples came, and said unto him, why speakest thou unto them in parables?
11) He answered and said unto them, "Because it is given unto you to know the mysteries of the kingdom of heaven, but to them it is not given.
12) For whosoever hath, to him shall be given, and he shall have more abundance: But whosoever hath not, from him shall be taken away even that he hath.
13) Therefore speak I to them in parables: Because they seeing see not; And hearing they hear not, neither do they understand.

14) And in them is fulfilled the prophecy of Esaias, which saith, by hearing ye shall hear, and shall not understand; and seeing ye shall see, and shall not perceive:
15) For this people's heart is waxed gross, and their ears are dull of hearing, and their eyes they have closed; Lest at any time they should see with their eyes, and hear with their ears, and should understand with their hearts, and should be converted, and I should heal them.
16) But blessed are your eyes, for they see: and your ears, for they hear.
17) For verily I say unto you, that many prophets and righteous men have desired to see those things which ye see, and have not seen them; And to hear those things which ye hear, and have not heard them.
18) Hear ye therefore the parable of the sower.
19) When any one heareth the word of the kingdom, and understandeth it not, then cometh the wicked one, and catcheth away that which was sown in his heart. This is he which received seed by the way side.
20) But he that received the seed into stony places, the same is he that heareth the word, and anon with joy receiveth it;
21) Yet hath he not root in himself, but dureth for while: For when tribulation or persecution ariseth because of the word, by and by he is offended.
22) He also that received seed among the thorns is he that heareth the word; And the care of this world, and the deceitfulness of riches, choke the word, and he becometh unfruitful.
23) But he that received seed into the good ground is he that heareth the word, and understandeth it; Which also beareth fruit, and bringeth forth, some an hundredfold, some sixty, some thirty".

The word is the good news of the life, death and resurrection of our Lord and savior Jesus Christ; And this word is what Jesus himself commissioned every follower of his to spread. The words of Jesus and his actions are the seeds that are to be sown. This is another one of the times that we must ask ourselves if we both believe Jesus as well as believing in him. I say this because as we have seen from lucifer in the Garden of Eden and his influence over the Pharisees, lucifer is very popular for undermining God's authority and making many believe that Jesus was not serious about the words he spoke or the seeds he planted. Lucifer is good at hiding his birds that are robbing the seeds dropped along the wayside. It does not surprise me either that the seeds that are obviously being plucked from people's understanding, just happen to be some big ones that greatly affect everyone that is trying to make it home to the Father.

When we hear the message of Jesus but do not understand his words or some of his commands, we begin to wonder and ask questions. This is the beginning of the asking and seeking process that we are commanded to undertake. Lucifer however, has those trapped in his system of thought that seek control and sell salvation and forgiveness. As the word begins to inspire us to seek and knock by asking questions, lucifer's birds pluck away the seed by saying that the sower was not serious about those seeds. Lucifer has been trying to discredit God's words from the beginning of time. Jesus was nothing but serious about our salvation and never joked about it. He knew his words were seeds planted for future generations and therefore did not give commandments or advice in jest.

One of the seeds that the wicked one snatches away when those being quickened by the Holy Ghost start asking, seeking and knocking, is in a story of Jesus being asked a question by a merchant. This is one of the seeds the wicked one plucks away by saying, "Oh, he wasn't serious when he said that". The lesson from this story is serious enough that it was allowed in the bible three different times by three different apostles. Each with the same reaction; "This is not possible", and since this story is all about how to enter heaven, of course lucifer does not want the masses to understand the complete lesson so he downplays it and teaches others to do the same.

Matthew 19:16-26

16) And, behold, one came and said unto him, good master, what good thing shall I do, that I may have eternal life?

17) And he said unto him, "Why callest thou me good? There is none good but one, that is, God: But if thou wilt enter into life, keep the commandments".

18) He saith unto him, which? Jesus said, "Thou shalt do no murder, thou shalt not commit adultery, thou shalt not steal, thou shalt not bear false witness,

19) Honor thy father and thy mother: And, thou shalt love thy neighbor as thyself".

20) The young man saith unto him, all these things have I kept from my youth up: What lack I yet?

21) Jesus said unto him, "If thou wilt be perfect, go and sell that thou hast, and give to the poor, and thou shalt have treasure in heaven: And come and follow me".

22) But when the young man heard that saying, he went away sorrowful: For he had great possessions.

23) Then said Jesus unto his disciples, "Verily I say unto you, that a rich man shall hardly enter into the kingdom of heaven.

24) And again I say unto you, it is easier for a camel to go through the eye of a needle, than for a rich man to enter into the kingdom of God".

25) When his disciples heard it, they were exceedingly amazed, saying, who then can be saved?

26) But Jesus beheld them, and said unto them, "With men this is impossible; But with God all things are possible".

Many find some of Jesus's words hard to take. It is usually easy to tell who has their magnets backwards because they are the ones pushing against Jesus the hardest, by ignoring his smallest commands and taking his words lightly and teaching others to do so, all so we feel better about not following his commands. Seems like there is a lot of this logic going on not just politically and personally but also religiously. If we believe the enemy that Jesus was only joking with this merchant or ruler and his apostles, why then was the response of the apostles in each telling one of shock? Did Jesus ever tell his apostles that he was only joking with the man? When we believe simply that Jesus was not serious, we allow the enemy to snatch the seed of understanding from a lesson we are to learn from this story. Asking and seeking would make us ask why he would say this. It is easy to shrug off especially if one thinks of a camel trying to go through the eye of an actual needle. Forgetting to take in the culture and land these events took place often misleads many to make wrong assumptions. Any merchant would have understood the words of Jesus if his heart was in the right place. Jesus lost the merchant at selling everything to give to the poor, therefore the merchant did not have ears for the rest and therefore had no understanding.

    In that land, there are mountain passes called the eye of the/a needle. In order for a merchant or wealthy man traveling with a lot of his wealth to go through, he must first unload his camel, walk the merchandise through by hand, then reload the camel on the other side after he walked the unloaded camel through the pass. In a way, it was still impossible for a camel to pass through while loaded. When we believe that Jesus was serious and we have the right information from asking and seeking, without truths being purposely withheld, we begin to understand that going through the eye of a needle is to pass into heaven; For the merchant's question was how he could enter heaven. In order to pass through, we have to learn to unpack our camels. We cannot pass through if we are trying to take it all with us. Jesus said these things because those that seek riches over the kingdom of heaven have a very hard time letting go when it comes time to go through the pass. We often end up doing all manner of selfishness just to hang onto the wealth we acquired. Many hold back truths to cater to the rich in fear of the collection plate drying up. This is where we get false teachings like faith equals prosperity or prosperity equals faith. Many don't seem to think that lucifer himself can promise wealth to those that bow to him and do his wickedness, or at the very least turn a blind eye to it all. Remember what he promised Jesus if he would only serve him?

    I once heard a wise man tell a story about how monkeys are sometimes caught. A box is made that can be anchored and it is filled with fruits and nuts that attract well. A hole is put in the front that is just big enough for a monkey to work his hand in to grab a handful of fruit and nuts. The monkeys want what is inside so bad that once they have their hand full, they cannot pull their hand back through the hole while holding the food. As the humans approach with the netting or tarp, the panic of the monkey overrides their ability to think to let go of the food. They never let go even as they are netted and captured. Does this sound about how the trickery of wealth makes many act? All the while looking down on those that choose not to reach into that hole knowing we might get trapped. It is all about perspective and I for one will do my best to learn Jesus's perspective.

  All any of us really need is food, shelter and water. Our lust and envy has caused us to store up more than what we need, putting our trust in our stored up wealth more than in our Heavenly Father. Our abundance along with our strive for power and success have made many of us forget why we were blessed to begin with. We ignore and forget the widows and orphans, the sick and the poor. Imagine if everyone was at least able to learn how to unpack their camel before passing. Jesus said how to do it. He did not say to give it to spoiled people that most times do not appreciate it or know how it was even made. He did not say to spend our wealth making new millionaires. He said to give it to the poor. Jesus also says that this is a way to gain riches in heaven, not that this should ever be our true goal. Imagine programs where people could donate their wealth as they unpack their camel, designed to help the different needs that would profit all, starting with the ones Jesus himself said we should be taking care of; Widows, orphans, the sick and the needy. Things like education and healthcare would be greatly boosted. Imagine leaders that truly served for the profit of all and not to line their own pockets. Positions of power and influence are corrupting because of this world being imperfect. So these positions should be held shortly so as to not allow any one person to become too corrupted. If one does not have the understanding of how a body works and has a heart to serve the broken and the poor, they should not even be allowed to hold positions. This is one of those lessons that if learned and applied, would show us a bit of what heaven would look like on earth, and it is possible or this exact saying would not be in the Lord's prayer. "Thy kingdom come, thy will be done, in earth as it is in heaven". It took a long time to get things this bad, it will take time to fix it, but it starts with learning and applying Jesus's lessons and his system of thought.

Here is a story of how a man that knows how to unpack his camel like Jesus meant, was able to help another in time of need.

2 Samuel 19:31-39

31) And Bar-zil'lai the Gileadite came down from Roge'lim, and went over Jordan with the king, to conduct him over Jordan.

32) Now Bar-zil'lai was a very aged man, even fourscore years old: And he had provided the king of sustenance while he lay at Ma-ha-na'im; For he was a very great man.

33) And the king said unto Bar-zil'lai, come thou over with me, and I will feed thee with me in Jerusalem.

34) And Bar-zil'lai said unto the king, how long have I to live, that I should go up with the king unto Jerusalem?

35) I am this day fourscore years old: And can I discern between good and evil? Can thy servant taste what I eat or what I drink? Can I hear any more the voice of singing men and singing woman? Wherefore then should thy servant be yet a burden unto my Lord the king?

36) Thy servant will go a little way over Jordan with the king and why should the king recompense it me with such a reward?

37) Let thy servant, I pray thee, turn back again, that I may die in mine own city, and be buried by the grave of my father and of my mother. But behold thy servant Chim'ham; Let him go over with my Lord the king; and do to him what shall seem good unto thee.

38) And the king answered, Chim'ham shall go over with me, and I will do to him that which shall seem good unto thee: And whatsoever thou shalt require of me, that will I do for thee.

39) And all the people went over Jordan. And when the king was come over, the king kissed Bar-zil'lai, and blessed him; And he returned unto his own place.

    Here is a perfect example of a man that is reading the signs of his own time. Someone that knew he could not take his wealth with him and knows how to approach the pass properly. Bar-zil'lai knew the lesson of unpacking his camel. He did not squander his wealth, but gave it to a good cause, to support the king on his journey home. This is merely one of many seeds that encourage us to overcome our own selfishness. To use what we are blessed with for the profit of all, especially before we attempt to go through the pass. This is one of many seeds that are taken up by the wayside. Robbed when we believe Jesus was not serious about his words. What we miss when we are convinced to not ask, seek and knock. I pray that many will see and understand the lesson of unpacking our camels, and the benefits this would have on all of humanity.

    Another seed that is plucked away when we are convinced that Jesus was not serious about his words, are words that even he admits are hard for some to receive. Many are either too soft hearted or stubborn to see what ignoring this lesson does to individuals and then a society. While the act of this lesson is not for every person, the lesson of it is however because it is ignoring this lesson that is to blame for allowing the suffering and defiling of God's little ones. We refuse to see what all Jesus was saying and the fact that he was instructing us on how to deal with certain matters. Again, we have to understand the culture and the things that were done to punish certain sins. We also fail to note in our eagerness to excuse all manner of wickedness, that Jesus did not condemn these things not once, he was teaching them to us.

Matthew 19:11,12

11) But he said unto them, "All men cannot receive this saying, save they to whom it is given.
12) For there are some eunuchs, which were so born from their mother's womb: And there are some eunuchs, which were made eunuchs of men: And there be eunuchs, which have made

themselves eunuchs for the kingdom of heaven's sake. He that is able to receive it, let him receive it".

Note that Jesus himself tells of the only three ways a eunuch is made that is acceptable to him, and if for him, then for God the Father also. He did not say anything about becoming a eunuch simply because we wanted to change our sex and live a wicked life. Too many forget or never learn the role many eunuchs played in many kingdoms and the ways Jesus said they were made. Those that ignore the words of Jesus and the apostles on these matters try to convince others that they were not serious about their instructions meant to help and guide not just us as individuals, but societies also. Instead, they invite in the unclean spirits that make them do the deeds of Sodom and Gomorrah. In Jesus's culture, He explains that some men are born as eunuchs, many of which dedicate themselves to God and temple service. Some men are made eunuchs by other men. Keep in mind in this culture, a man had his hand cut off for stealing. The punishment fits the crime. These are the men rapists and the ones guilty of sexual abominations like abusing children and teaching them to do the same. They had the source of their problem removed. Then there are the men that make themselves eunuchs. These men do this for one of two reasons. They either make themselves eunuchs merely to dedicate their lives to serving God only, or they make themselves eunuchs because they know and fear a wicked desire within themselves, and keep in mind the difference between the sinful which we all are, and the wicked, which we all are not. These last eunuchs understood and believed the words of Jesus and the apostles. Because of their choice, many that dedicated themselves to God's service that had sexual battles within themselves, did not go on to abuse women or God's little ones.

Matthew 5:27-30

27) "Ye have heard that it was said by them of old time, thou shalt not commit adultery:

28)   But I say unto you, that whosoever looketh on a woman to lust after her hath committed adultery with her already in his heart.

29)   And if thy right eye offend thee, pluck it out, and cast it from thee: For it is profitable for thee that one of thy members should perish, and not that thy whole body should be cast into hell.

30)   And if thy right hand offend thee, cut it off, and cast it from thee: For it is profitable for thee that one of thy members should perish, and not that thy whole body should be cast into hell".

Mark 9:43-48

43)   "And if thy hand offend thee, cut it off: It is better for thee to enter into life maimed, than having two hands to go into hell, into the fire that never shall be quenched:

44)   where their worm dieth not, and the fire is not quenched.

45)   And if thy foot offend thee, cut it off: It is better for thee to enter halt into life, than having two feet to be cast into hell, into the fire that never shall be quenched:

46)   Where their worm dieth not, and the fire is not quenched.

47)   And if thine eye offend thee, Pluck it out: It is better for thee to enter into the kingdom of God with one eye, than having two eyes to be cast into hell fire:

48)   Where their worm dieth not, and the fire is not quenched".

This is usually when the argumentative would blow a gasket. Before anyone does, read Isaiah and be reminded that Eunuchs did have a role and their own blessing.

Isaiah 56:1-5

1)   Thus saith the Lord, keep ye judgement, and do justice: for my salvation is near to come, and my righteousness to be revealed.

2) Blessed is the man that layeth hold on it; that keepeth the sabbath from polluting it, and keepeth his hand from doing any evil.

3) Neither let his son of the stranger, that hath joined himself to the Lord, speak, saying, the Lord hath utterly seperated me from his people: neither let the Eunuch say, behold, I am a dry tree.

4) For thus saith the Lord unto the Eunuchs that keep my sabbaths and choose the things that please me, and take hold of my covenant:

5) Even unto them will I give in mine house and within my walls a place and a name better than of sons and of daughters: I will give them an everlasting name, that shall not be cut off.

One can definitely see where many would not take these words of Jesus seriously. Especially when one does not know the laws and punishments of the culture. Many fail to remember that Jesus grew up around these laws and did not say they were bad. Instead, he uses them in his teachings and we ignore them. Again, in his culture a man had a hand cut off that was caught stealing, so there were a lot of maimed individuals in his time because the punishment fit the crime. I am not saying that we should poke our eye out because we looked at a man or woman. These higher punishments were for those that had a habitual problem. Many with lucifer's system of thought love to argue so much that they will ignore these differences. They were perpetual offenders that simply could not stop themselves. Things like lust are a bigger problem in our days since evil has many more ways to push it on society than in Jesus's day. One way to "pluck" out our eye when dealing with lust problems is to first get rid of the visual devices we use to see it. Some may have to go as far as to quit watching T.V. and stay away from computers that give access. Some might even have to downgrade their phones so they cannot look stuff up. As far as avoiding the opposite sex that dress like harlots in public, one would have to live with their heads looking up or simply move into the wilderness. Even today's society would consider these simple solutions to be too much to ask unfortunately. Many of us are not even willing to do one of these things to avoid our selfish desires. This is also one of the reasons why God gave us marriage. Ignoring these next instructions is why we see so many marriages fail, and why we see ones like priests who say they dedicated themselves to Jesus and his teachings, ignore his instructions and find themselves paying the price by defiling God's little ones.

1 Corinthians 7:1-9

1)   Now concerning the things whereof ye wrote unto me: It is good for a man not to touch a woman.
2)   Nevertheless, to avoid fornication, let every man have his own wife, and let every woman have her own husband.
3)   Let the husband render unto the wife due benevolence: And likewise also the wife unto the husband.
4)   The wife hath not power of her own body, but the husband: And likewise also the husband hath not power of his own body, but the wife.
5)   Defraud ye not one the other, except it be with consent for a time, that ye may give yourselves to fasting and prayer; And come together again, that satan tempt you not for your incontinency.
6)   But I speak this by permission, and not of commandment.
7)   For I would that all men were even as I myself. But every man hath his proper gift of God, one after this manner, and another after that.
8)   I say therefore to the unmarried and widows, it is good for them if they abide even as I.
9)   But if they cannot contain, let them marry: <u>For it is better to marry than to burn.</u>

So many these days blame God the Father for all of the things created by our choice of actions. We ignore the commands and advice of Jesus and the apostles given in scripture, beat others over the head with scriptures we choose to look at, then blame everyone but ourselves for how those choices not only corrupt our own lives, but the lives of future generations. It continues passing from one generation to another until nobody even realizes things are so bad, much less how we got where we are at. Then we harden our hearts so we do not have to feel responsible and never hear the Holy Ghost trying to tell us that Jesus's system of thought is the way back, and lucifer's is how we got here. We ignore Jesus and the Apostle Paul, then wonder why so many fall to the selfishness of lust. We wonder why even priests are defiling God's little ones. What used to be done to fight against our evil lusts is twisted and used to defile further. These evil and weak actions and thoughts are being taught to God's innocent ones and Jesus is clear on his thoughts on this.

Mark 9:42
42)   "And whosoever shall offend one of these little ones that believe in me, it is better for him that a millstone were hanged about his neck, and he were cast into the sea".

   It is no mistake that Jesus gives this warning the same time that he is instructing on adultery and the ways a eunuch is made. Anyone that abuses children that believe in him, especially sexually, and teaches others to do the same is not thought of very highly by Jesus. Jesus and the apostles understood how and why we were created. They understood that we were designed to populate the earth so his plan of salvation could unfold, therefore the need or desire to procreate is built into us. Many might ask why then did God forbid Adam and Eve from eating the fruit. Simple really. God knew the nature of his creations, both Adam and Eve as well as lucifer. As in all of his commands to not do something, he was drawing out lucifer's system of thought for all to see knowing that lucifer's defiant nature would trick humanity into doing it. God obviously built Adam and Eve to reproduce or they would not have been able to after they were kicked out of the garden. What better way to make something happen than to tell everyone not to do it. He even built Adam with the yearning because God witnessed this yearning in Adam as he named all of the animals. It wasn't until after God saw this that he said it was not good for man to be alone. So after Adam had named every animal God created, He caused Adam to fall asleep and then made Eve. How long does one think it took Adam to name every animal God made on the planet? Genesis 2:18-25.

    God knew of our selfish nature and the evil desires of many. So he gave us instructions for marriage and how to address the evil lusts that some have. God knows that lucifer uses our desires against us as he tricks us to believe that Jesus and the apostles were not serious about their words. Many that do abominable things use the excuse that they were born that way, ignoring Jesus's instructions that we have to be born again to enter heaven, and born again means a change. Too many forget that as helpmates, we are to help each other against the temptations we each face every time we leave our homes. Unfortunately we do not even have the safety of our own home anymore, as they each have a window capable of spewing filth in every room and even in every hand. The Apostle Paul warns against spouses withholding affection except for reasons of spiritual fasting. Yet affection is used like a child being abused in a custody battle. Then so many wonder why marriages do not last anymore. Spouses are sending each other into a war zone each day with no weapon or ammo to resist the temptations targeted at us all daily. "My people perish from lack of knowledge." Yet we never stop or slow enough to see our own part in making others fall. As long as we keep getting the addictions we want and our own desires, most do not even care even though they claim to love the one they are with, selfishness truly does blind. All of this because we are taught to not take certain scriptures seriously, yet ignoring them has such a huge impact on us again as both individuals and as a society. All because the seeds planted are plucked away before we finish the process of asking, seeking and knocking.

    This particular seed that is missed due to lucifer and his system of thought is why marriages and sexuality are being twisted. Ignoring scriptural instructions is why society is being hijacked by those pushing lucifer's system of thought on all of humanity, with children as their target audience. The wicked seem to have learned what Christians are moving too fast to remember, that our youth are the next generations and the key to future change. We miss these seeds when we refuse to read for ourselves and trust in those that defile little ones because they themselves ignore the scriptures, making big deals out of the smallest things while ignoring the major things. Lucifer has the world moving so fast that the majority do not see the speed that sexuality has been pushed in such a short time. It is true that there is nothing new under the sun. That there is no temptation today that they did not have then. The difference is the percentage of people that believe in modesty and understand and respect our natural design and purpose. With a growing population taught to disrespect sexuality and each other, a man or woman trying to be faithful almost has to walk around with their head looking up, all because self respect and self control are no longer taught and expected any more.

    How many remember the movie Splash with Tom Hanks? The old movie about a mermaid? For those that do not, in the beginning of the movie there are two young boys on a ship. One of the boys purposely drops coins so he can take a peek under a woman's long dress. He literally had to put his head to the floor to look up her dress. Did she want a child to look at her small clothes? No, that is why the dress covered her body somewhat properly. This shows that one, there will always be those that are eager to see more than they should, even children. Two, that modesty not only keeps those unwanted eyes from seeing, but that those that still try, have to work harder at it which brings obvious attention to their attempts.

    Unfortunately, in this day and age that is rapidly being shaped into the image of Sodom and Gomorrah, young boys do not have to drop things or use trickery to see what they want anymore. They do not even have to peek in ladies rooms or go to beaches. Sadly, at times, they see what they want in stores, schools and even in what should be called houses of prayer. Society has allowed itself to become so desensitized with our lusts that we become blind to what is being pushed on younger generations, and its consequences. We allow our young children to become sexualized at early ages. We allow our young ladies to dress in ways to attract then put them together with young men at their most sexually frustrated ages, then blame their attention problem on things like hair color or facial hair. We ignore the instructions for marriage and wonder why teachers and coaches are lusting after the children we allow to dress in ways to attract any eye filled with lust. We want our children to learn but we allow the world and lucifer's system of thought to corrupt them and keep them distracted. Unfortunately this infection bleeds into our adult life as well.

    In a society that seems to encourage every deadly sin because of personal profit, men and women forget the importance and need for modesty. Especially women these days it seems, even though it is men's lustful desires that women are catering to. Many feel like it is for their own happiness that they dress to please the eyes of others, somehow thinking that the ones they dress loosely for are the only ones that can and do see them. When in fact, even in this, they are being manipulated for corporate profits like so many other things that have to do with their body and choice. Women no longer wait for the bedroom to wear what only their husband should see, but now walk around in public casting their pearls before not only swine, but innocent young eyes also, then simply laugh about it. Women sometimes become so lost and distracted in their desire to look good for either themselves or whoever they are baiting, that they overlook the stumbling block they become for married men trying to do right by their wives, or young men trying to hold out for marriage to receive blessings and yes, even young innocent minds that do not need help building their spank bank that modern cartoons start for them. The saddest and most selfish part is that these same women try to excuse this behavior by saying that it is their right and choice to be able to dress this way, and we should feel bad for even saying anything. I would say what about the rights and choices of those children and adults rescued from sex trafficking? Do they not have the right to walk in public without seeing sights of sexuality that triggers the traumas they faced? Does it not make it hard on those raised in sexual abuse to control any appetites that this abuse caused and/or created? Many are fighting battles that others have no clue of, yet only women have the rights that matter? The selfish logic of it is ridiculous.

Let all of this sink in for those that like to wear workout pants or even breastfeed in public exposing themselves fully. In a non sexualized world these things would not be a problem. There are even tribes of people that can live in an almost all naked community, but they do not teach sexuality like America does. That is the difference. But this society is highly sexualized to the point of looking like Sodom and Gomorrah, and we dress in public like the majority of minds have not been corrupted. We may convince ourselves that this is not an issue, but I assure anyone that it is, and we all will be held accountable for purposely making innocent victims stumble. Parents will be held accountable for raising children wearing shorts letting the world of swine see their child's butt cheeks hanging out. When did parents become the dealer for eye candy for pedophiles? Ignoring the truth does not make it false and it certainly does not work as an excuse for Jesus. In a harlot's mind, the unclean spirits they harbor would have them say, "married men should not look then". I am guessing children must wear blinds in public also. It amazes me how selfishness will make us bend the rights of others just to justify one's desire to dress like a harlot in public. We ignore the fact that we were made with the need and desire to go forth and multiply. We ignore the fact that God and the apostles knew this as well and is why we have instructions to help in our daily battles. It should become apparent why there are dangers to believers living among non believers, especially when the number of non believers become the majority. We are seeing these effects in our voting system now. This truth is exactly how we get plagued with too many snakes in the hen house.

As some might be able to tell, This topic is close to my heart because I was a child that was introduced to things like porn and sexual activity at a very young age. I had my battles throughout my life because of those influences, until Jesus taught me to put down the chains that his death unlocked.

These battles helped me to see and understand the problem for what it is, and how it is decaying our society from the inside out as it did with Sodom and Gomorrah. All one has to do is be still and watch where people's eyes go. If it was not a huge issue, the porn industry would not be a billion dollar industry.
Trafficking would not be a record growing industry itself that targets young innocent boys and girls. But here we are, still looking in a mirror before leaving the house, only caring about how our outfit makes our butt or breasts stand out. Good going, I'm sure little 10 year olds that have too much internet access, as well as those filthy industries that you're giving kids the appetite for appreciate it very much. I know for a fact that lucifer and his unclean spirits who are looking for innocence to cling to do. These industries appreciate spouses that ignore the scriptures and withhold affection because it pushes most to watch the very industries that are providing the outlet for the sexual trafficking of innocence. Yes, it can be said that our selfishness to refuse our partner helps support the porn and trafficking industry, and yes, the next sexual video some might watch may be starring a sexually trafficked child that could be someones missing child. let this also sink in.

    Do these truths make one's demons feel uncomfortable? I pray wholeheartedly that it is like salt in a wound for them. Because our society, especially in these last days, has become too blindly eager to serve unclean spirits and satisfy our lustful flesh and corporate profits. Even at the cost of corrupting our future generations. We oversexualize our children, never teaching them responsibility and the power of self control. Instead we allow those that profit from it to incourage premarital sex. Even to the point of promoting murder as a form of birth control, because murder is to kill for selfish reasons and any abortion done not for medical reasons is for selfish reasons. This teaches our children to slack on obligation, responsibility and self control as well as injecting a disrespect for life that will slowly get worse over the generations, until all of humanity no longer cares for life. We then wonder why we have so many rapists, child molesters or just sexually confused. We put rapists and pedophiles in prisons that do nothing but worsen these appetites just to let them out again with no change, all because the prison system is broken and corrupt itself and does not care to help them change so they do not return, again because there is no money in cures. All of this once again because we let the seeds meant to help us be plucked away before we have a chance to understand. We pull God out of every aspect of our lives in America thinking we can keep any protection and blessings that he gave us. We have become so blinded by selfishness that we do not even see the full depths of it. We do not even see that America is becoming the whore in Revelation.

    The fix to this is not easy and I am not sure that we are not already past the point of no return. As in sports psychology, to fix or change anything that has been made a habit, society as a whole has to slow back down to learning speed in order to successfully make a habitual change. Changes in a habit cannot be made at full speed and lucifer knows this. That is why he pushes society to move faster and faster as we chase our selfishness more and more. Leaving our next generations to be shaped and molded by a system of thought that belongs to the father of lies. Jesus gave us the key in the Lord's prayer when he prayed for the Father to give us "this day" our daily bread. Again, he did not ask for this week or this month, but this day. Moving faster than one day at a time creates many of the societal issues we see today, because moving too fast opens up many doors for lucifer and his. Jesus then gave us the other key in John 3:14,15. Many of us miss it because we let John 3:16 overshadow it, 14 and 15 is Jesus pointing the way back to a story in Numbers 21. The story of Moses and His people. Jesus is letting us know that when things get too bad in our own lives or even in society itself, the only true reset button is to slow back down and turn our eyes back to him and his teachings. His system of thought is the only successful reset for the selfishness that dominates our world.

    I pray that we as a society would slow down to fix our bad habits before it has to be done for us, like what has had to be done so many times before in history with God's people. For we know that if we do not learn from history, we become doomed to repeat it and God says that his people perish from lack of knowledge. Notice that the mistakes of God's people are not taught in schools? Who would want mankind to continue those mistakes? We are dangerously close to a whole world that is proudly performing the deeds of Sodom and Gomorrah, and we all know, or should know, how that displeased God and what he did about it. Genesis 19:1-29. How much God will endure can be seen in that story and can be used as a sign of the times. For when the whole world is doing the deeds of Sodom and Gomorrah, we are nearing the end. The question for many of us is, were we a part of the fight against it or a part of the problem spreading it? And I do not believe that sitting on the sideline is accepted in the end. Jesus says that there will be much wailing and gnashing of teeth. Many good people will wonder why they were turned away. So do we continue to let lucifer's birds steal the sower's seeds that are meant to wake us up and help us in our battles? Because if we continue to believe that Jesus and the apostles were not serious about their advice and commands, society will continue to spiral out of control just like lucifer wants, because misery loves company.

    The seed stolen away that touches me deeply is the one we miss in the story of the prodigal son. The seed in this story is missed often, once again, because those that are under lucifer's control like the Scribes and the Pharisees, tell anyone that tries to ask and seek that, "oh, he wasn't serious when he said that".

Matthew 23:9,10

9)   "And call no man your father upon the earth: For one is your father, which is in heaven.

10)   Neither be ye called masters: For one is your master, even Christ".

1 John 2:3,4

3)   And hereby we do know that we know Him, if we keep his commandments.

4)   He that saith, I know Him, and keepeth not his commanments, is a liar, and the truth is not in him.

Notice that God used a command to not do something in the garden to draw lucifer's system of thought out? Jesus does the same here as he once again commands us not to do something. It really does amaze me that only about 400 years or so after Jesus said these words, a system of thought influenced by lucifer that is similar to the Pharisees decides to call themselves what Jesus said not to, then when asked about it, their best answer is, "oh, he wasn't serious when he said that". Sounds a bit too much like, "you won't surely die" for my liking. They not only disobey a direct command from Jesus himself by calling themselves father, they even use the title holy father themselves. Then many of them ignore the scriptural instructions of the Apostle Paul to marry in order not to burn in lust. Many think they can defeat the God given desire to reproduce and therefore burn in lust for it as their desire spirals out of control having them defile God's innocent ones, rather than repenting of their weakness and following scriptural instructions on the matter. Then when they make a habit of it after justifying it in their twisted faith by this time, they further ignore Jesus's lesson about eunuchs. All because they ignore God's word and teach others to do the same, all while stealing the sower's seed. When we are told that Jesus was not serious by those we are supposed to trust, most of us do not ask about it anymore. We stop seeking and knocking for an answer. When we stop searching and allow ourselves to be misled, we allow lucifer to steal the seed meant for our good, for the profit of all. I do not recall a single time that Jesus was not serious about our salvation or how to obtain it. Everything that Jesus said and did was for a reason. He knew that his words and actions would be echoed throughout time. Lucifer is the one that has been demeaning God's words and instructions since the creation.

    To understand why Jesus would tell us to call no man father on earth, for we have one father which is in heaven, we also need to understand the reasons he came. Jesus came to pay the price for the law of sacrifice that bridges the gap for humanity to be forgiven through belief in Jesus. Jesus's sacrifice pays for the selfishness of humanity. The words and teachings of Jesus were to be our example. Jesus was teaching us what heaven will be like. This is why many of his lessons started out with him saying that, "heaven is like". Jesus even teaches what the judgment process will be like since he will be our judge. Jesus spent a lot of time showing us the nature of God the Father. He tells us that if we know him then we know the Father. Knowing that Jesus wants to introduce us to the Father helps us to understand why he would tell us to call no man on earth father. Especially after we read some of his lessons and parables that mention a father or master. Jesus is wanting us to not only learn from these parables by putting ourselves in place of the main characters, which gives us a worldly understanding of the stories. But Jesus also wants us to understand it from a spiritual perspective. He wants us to put God the Father as the character in these parables and we are the ones in the story causing him problems. We learn the parables from the perspective of God the Father and what he goes through with us his children. Jesus is once again introducing us to God the Father when we seek and find these connections as the Holy Ghost opens the door of understanding to us. Unfortunately, the door never opens if we believe that, "he wasn't serious when he said that".

Take the prodigal son story for example.

Luke 15:11-32

11) And he said, " A certain man had two sons:

12) And the younger of them said to his Father, Father, give me the portion of goods that falleth to me. And he divided unto them his living.

13) And not many days after the younger son gathered all together, and took his journey into a far country, and there wasted his substance with riotous living.

14) And when he had spent all, there arose a mighty famine in the land; And he began to be in want.

15) And he went and joined himself to a citizen of that country; And he sent him into his fields to feed swine.

16) And he would fain have filled his belly with the husks that the swine did eat: And no man gave unto him.

17) And when he came to himself, he said, how many hired servants of my Father's have bread enough and to spare, and I perish with hunger!
18) I will arise and go to my Father, and will say unto him, Father, I have sinned against heaven, and before thee,
19) And am no more worthy to be called thy son: Make me as one of thy hired servants.
20) And he arose, and came to his Father. But when he was yet a great way off, his Father saw him, and had compassion, and ran, and fell on his neck, and kissed him.
21) And the son said unto him, Father, I have sinned against heaven, and in thy sight, and am no more worthy to be called thy son.
22) But the Father said to his servants, bring forth the best robe, and put it on him; And put a ring on his hand, and shoes on his feet:
23) And bring hither the fatted calf, and kill it; And let us eat, and be merry:
24) For this my son was dead, and is alive again; He was lost, and is found. And they began to be merry.
25) Now his elder son was in the field: And as he came and drew nigh to the house, he heard musick and dancing.
26) And he called one of the servants, and asked what these things meant.
27) And he said unto him, thy brother is come; And thy Father hath killed the fatted calf, because he hath received him safe and sound.
28) And he was angry, and would not go in: Therefore came his Father out, and intreated him.
29) And he answering said to his Father, lo, these many years do I serve thee, neither transgressed I at any time thy commandment: And yet thou never gavest me a fatted calf, that I might make merry with my friends:
30) But as soon as thy son was come, which hath devoured thy living with harlots, thou hast killed for him the fatted calf.
31) And he said unto him, son, thou art ever with me, and all that I have is thine.

32) It was meet that we should make merry, and be glad: For this thy brother was dead, and is alive again; And was lost, and is found".

There are lessons in the parables Jesus told and what lesson we understand depends on where our hearts are at. Those truly asking and seeking will understand while those with an argumentative and denying heart will not. This is a big reason why it is important to read the bible throughout our lives. Even if we only understand a small portion now, life experiences help the Holy Ghost unlock our understanding. For example, What we might not understand before having children, we may understand after. There is no reading the bible once and understanding all, it is not made that way. It is not made for any one man to understand all, this is what makes us need each other like pieces of a puzzle, only someone is trying to hide critical pieces. Where our heart is at plays the biggest role in our understanding though. If our heart is not in the right place, understanding will never be ours. That is the importance of the walk with Jesus. That walk continuously changes our hearts, opening up new understandings as we go. Even the apostles wondered why Jesus spoke in parables.

Matthew 13:10-15

10) And the disciples came, and said unto him, why speakest thou unto them in parables?
11) He answered and said unto them, "Because it is given unto you to know the mysteries of the kingdom of heaven, but to them it is not given.
12) For whosoever hath, to him shall be given, and he shall have more abundance: But whosoever hath not, From him shall be taken away even that he hath.
13) Therefore speak I to them in Parables: Because they seeing see not; And hearing they hear not, Neither do they understand.
14) And in them is fulfilled the prophecy of Esaias, which saith, by hearing ye shall hear, and shall not understand; And seeing ye shall see, and shall not perceive.

15) For this people's heart is waxed gross, and their eyes they have closed; lest at any time they should see with their eyes, and hear with their ears, and should understand with their heart, and should be converted, and I should heal them".

It is no wonder that Jesus speaks these words before warning us about his seeds/lessons being stolen away by the wicked one and his system of thought.

Matthew 13:19

19) 'When any one heareth the word of the kingdom, and understandeth it not, then cometh the wicked one, and catcheth away that which was sown in his heart. This is he which received seed by the wayside".

Many of us understand the prodigal son story from an earthly perspective, especially if we have been in one of the three positions mentioned in the story; The spoiled son that wanted his inheritance early, the prideful son or the Father that has children that will not get along due to the selfishness they all carry. When we ask and seek why Jesus says to call no man father, then tells us parables using that title, we understand that he is also introducing us to the problem that our Father in Heaven was faced with. When we see this story from the eyes of our Father in Heaven, we can see the reason he needed a plan to reconcile his two groups of children. We see that the Father cannot have peace in his kingdom until he can reconcile his sons, and this cannot happen until his children see the selfishness that is causing the war and division and contention.

As we see and understand this story through the Father's eyes, other seeds stand out shedding light on the two groups of children.

John 1:11,12

11) He came unto his own, and his own received him not.
12) But as many as received him, to them gave he power to become the sons of God, even to them that believe on his name:

Jesus came to his own but was crucified because of their pride. Note in the prodigal son story that the prideful son wanted nothing to do with the wayward son. The prideful son did not think that the Father should let the wayward son come home. Does this sound familiar? Does this sound like how the Jews see Gentiles? The Jews saw Gentiles as dogs and treated them as so. It took a lowly Gentile woman for the spirit to show even Jesus that the plan of salvation included the Gentiles, making the Gentiles the wayward sons and the Jews the prideful sons.

Matthew 15:21-28

21) Then Jesus went thence, and departed into the coasts of Tyre and Si'don.
22) And, behold, a woman of Canaan came out of the same coasts, and cried unto him, saying, have mercy on me, o Lord, thou son of David; My daughter is grievously vexed with a devil.
23) But he answered her not a word. And his disciples came and besought him, saying, send her away; for she crieth after us.
24) But he answered and said, "I am not sent but unto the lost sheep of the house of Israel".
25) then came she and worshipped him, saying, Lord, help me.
26) But he answered and said, "It is not meet to take the children's bread, and to cast it to dogs".
27) And she said, truth, Lord: Yet the dogs eat of the crumbs which fall from their master's table.
28) Then Jesus answered and said unto her, "o woman, great is thy faith: Be it unto thee even as thou wilt". And her daughter was made whole from that very hour.

The plan is two fold, create a place where both the prideful and spoiled children can live with free will. Free to act out any selfish thought or desire. Freedom to do any manner of good or evil over a time frame that will undeniably show us all what our selfishness creates without the Father. In time, even the prideful Jews will see through Jesus's death, that even they are eaten up with selfishness outside of the Father's presence. When both Jew and Gentile see the full extent of what our selfishness breeds, what the sins we allowed our selfishness to create has done to God's creation, the understanding of why we needed Jesus to make the sacrifice none of us could satisfy will start to manifest. The plan to reconcile both Jew and Gentile through the blood of Jesus the Christ; To reconcile the prideful children back with the spoiled, all so there can be peace in the kingdom once more doesn't seem like it is too far fetched, when we see things through the eyes of the Father. Yet lucifer works hard to keep all of the Father's children infected with selfishness that breeds the sins destroying everything. Lucifer is adept at corrupting even those meant to guide with his system of thought, as we learn with the Scribes and Pharisees. As lucifer has done from the beginning, he either hides and changes truth and law or he tricks us into believing that the bible isn't serious. Which is like a bird robbing the seed dropped by the wayside. Once we understand that the plan is to reconcile both Jew and Gentile, we can see all of the ways lucifer tries to stop this by the divisions he creates. Again, this understanding shows glimpses into why lucifer works so hard to keep the body seperate and at war with each other, not just in the religious body either. We see the insane amounts of pride that he injects the world with trying to make it all fall. We understand why we are told the story of Esau selling his birthright to his brother Jacob for stew in Genesis 25:29-34. Lucifer teaches prosperity equals faith to get us to sell our birthright in heaven for wealth on earth. We also start to sympathize with God the Father and all we have put him through. We can start to understand how all of Jesus's lessons were to prepare us for the look in the mirror that it takes for us to see our selfishness. We start seeing the poetry in motion that is the Holy Ghost working hard to fulfill the Father's plan of salvation for all that would believe in his plan. Then maybe we will understand better the Apostle Paul's lesson in 1 Corinthians 12.

    I pray that we would not allow the wicked one to trick us into not asking or seeking. I pray that the Holy Ghost would not let us fall for the same tricks lucifer used on Eve in the garden. I pray that denominations, governments and cultures would learn the lesson of there being diversities of gifts, but the same spirit; differences of administrations, but the same Lord; And diversities of operations, but the same God. The lesson that every action and word is meant to be for the profit of all, not just a select few. This is the magnet that humanity has backwards that is flooding this world with lucifer's influence, with his selfishness. The sooner we learn these lessons the sooner we all become better at fulfilling the great commission given to all by Jesus. The sooner the body parts stop throwing stones at each other, fighting over Jesus's spot; The sooner the body will snap back together and be whole again in harmony. I pray wholeheartedly that the sower's seed would not be stolen by the wicked one, and that through our asking, seeking and knocking, we would see the spirit's poetry in motion that creates the story of Jesus working and healing through us all. I pray that we will see that we are worshiping Jesus when we do what he commands, being kind and loving to all, treating others as we ourselves wish to be treated, forgiving as we wish our Father in heaven to forgive us and even the simple commands to not call ourselves father is a form of obeying and therefore worships God. That we worship lucifer every time that we give in to our evil selfish desires, every time we disobey the smallest command and teach others to do the same. That we let either good or evil influence and touch this world through our actions and words, and these actions and words show our fruits to all. May we strive for good fruits so that we may become better stewards to be used by our Father in heaven.

    Finally, I pray that we all learn the lesson Jesus references in John 3:14, of what his people had to do to overcome the serpent's venom in Numbers 21. To survive the selfish venom of lucifer, humanity has to keep their eyes on the son of God which was sacrificed to be the way, the truth and the life for all that would believe.

THE GREAT COMMISSION

The first questions that many ask is, what is the great commission; Who gave it and who did they give it to? The answer is easily found in many of the books in the new testament. The great commission is simply the last words and commands that Jesus gave to his apostles before ascending into heaven. Jesus gave this commission to all followers of his because it is the entire body of Christ that is commissioned. Each body part or member is given specific gifts to profit all other parts/members in this work. Here are two accounts of the great commission that are simple in my opinion.

Matthew 28:18-20
18) And Jesus came and spake unto them, saying, "All power is given unto me in heaven and in earth.
19) Go ye therefore, and teach all nations, baptizing them in the name of the Father, and of the Son, and of the Holy Ghost.
20) Teaching them to observe all things whatsoever I have commanded you: And, lo, I am with you alway, even unto the end of the world. Amen".

Mark 16:15-18
15) And he said unto them, "Go ye into all the world, and preach the gospel to every creature.
16) He that believeth and is baptized shall be saved; But he that believeth not shall be damned.
17) And these signs shall follow them that believe; In my name shall they cast out devils; they shall speak with new tongues;
18) They shall take up serpents; And if they drink any deadly thing, it shall not hurt them; They shall lay hands on the

sick, and they shall recover".

These are the last words of Jesus spoken here on earth to his followers, his words. I emphasize "his" words, because it appears there is a question we all need to ask ourselves from time to time. Do we merely believe in Jesus or do we believe his words also? I mention this a lot because Jesus makes it clear that belief is important. Our level of belief in not only Jesus, but in his words also, directly influences our ability and/or desire to work towards fulfilling the great commission. It also affects our ability to work well with different administrations and operations that were given different gifts for the different ways to help the whole body of Christ. It poses a curious question of how many innocent people were killed as "witches", merely for using one of the spiritual gifts mentioned by the Apostle Paul, all because those under lucifer's system of thought did not take the scriptures seriously unless it suited their sinful desires for wealth and power. How many were allowed to be killed because these same religious leaders withheld proper teaching, that would have kept people from mistaking spiritual gifts for witchcraft?

The only proof we need to see that many are not believing in Jesus's words, is in those that do not believe that baptism is an ingredient in our salvation. If his own words are not enough to teach us the importance of baptism, his own actions should be. If baptism is not needed, why did a sinless man show us the example then later command us all to do the same? So why then do we allow lucifer to convince so many that Jesus was not serious about his words and joked about our salvation? We often forget that lucifer does not need help tripping mankind in our own selfish desires. Lucifer works hard to twist God's words teaching mankind to make light of God's instructions, all to step into God's authority. So we have to continually ask ourselves if we truly believe the words of Jesus himself, or do we only go through the motions we are taught merely saying we believe in him? Because as we teach our children, actions are louder than words.

Another question that arises as we strive to fulfill the commission Jesus gave is, Do we sometimes hinder others in their mission to fulfill the great commission in their own lives? I believe we do, and luckily we are not alone in this matter. The bible tells of Jesus's apostles doing this very thing. The mistake is recorded twice and is to show us that even the apostles can make mistakes and become too eager to judge and forbid. Let us not think that we are better than even the apostles.

Mark 9:38-40

38) And John answered him, saying, we saw one casting out devils in thy name, and he followeth not us: And we forbade him, because he followeth not us.
39) But Jesus said, "Forbid him not: For there is no man which shall do a miracle in my name, that can lightly speak evil of me.
40) For he that is not against us is on our part".

Again, do we believe the words of Jesus himself? Too often we allow lucifer to catch us up being so eager to judge others, that we make the very mistake the apostles made. We become blind to the Holy Ghost working in and through the lives of others. Just like the apostles that forbad a man that was doing the very same work that they were called to do. They did not take the time to slow down and look at the man's fruits first. They did not know this man, yet he was a product of Jesus's ministry. To the apostles, this man casting out devils in Jesus's name was a nobody. They forbade him because they thought they were the only one with the authority to do the works of God, sound familiar? I honestly believe that this was an eye opening experience for the apostles, they merely had to be rebuked so they could see the errors of their logic that would lead to the scattering of the flock, not gathering.

Too often the progress of the great commission is slowed due to unbelief in the words of Jesus. Our selfishness is quick to help our unbelief, and together the 2 cloud our judgment making us do the very things we are commanded not to. In our haste, we throw stones at any member of the body that is, "not with us". This lesson that we tend to forget often is not solely for the denominations that are the members making up the body of Christ, which are its believers. This lesson is true for anything that can be considered a body, from a group of friends to businesses, governments and even whole cultures. Like any body, it will slowly go down hill as long as each part throws stones only being concerned with their own profit. The body thrives when the members put down their stones and stop fighting over Jesus's spot, the head, and thinks for the profit of all.

    The great commission is to teach the world who Jesus is and every single thing that he did for all humanity. To tell of his promises along with the words and actions that he left us all as the perfect example, along with sharing what Jesus has done in our own lives through the Holy Ghost to encourage and inspire, helping us all endure to the end. We become living testimonies of the truths that Jesus spoke. We become living stones being used to build his church on earth as it is in heaven which is a whole people not merely a building made with human hands. It is then baptizing all who believe so the Holy Ghost can start working in our lives, using our gifts and talents to reach even further, spider webbing like poetry in motion until his message and teachings spread to all the world. Until all have had a chance to accept or deny the gift of salvation and forgiveness for humanity's selfishness against our Father in Heaven.

    I for one believe the words of my Lord and savior Jesus Christ, and I believe that the Holy Ghost is using my gifts and occupations, that he inspires, to spread the message that often, we get our magnets backwards in our eagerness to forbid others. In doing this, we push away from the body of Christ as we fight over Jesus's position. I pray that in the end, we will be seen more eager to spread his words which we believe than judging harshly and forbidding one another. May we ask ourselves at the end of each day, did I do more sharing of Jesus today than I did forbidding and judging? Because we are worshiping the Father when we believe Jesus by doing the things he commanded us to do as well as not doing what we are told not to do. We worship lucifer when we continue to work against the whole body. Obedience is a huge part of worship and the question is, who are we obeying, Jesus or lucifer? Actions are louder than words. I pray that we learn that worshiping and fulfilling the great commission is an everyday thing, not just a once a week or sometimes thing. May the Holy Ghost continue to shape, mold and guide us to be the best tools we can be in the work to fulfill Jesus's great commission. I pray that we become strong enough in faith to not break in his hands as we do the works to complete the great commission. Finally, I pray we will understand that we all need the shaping and molding process to change our hearts, so that we can survive his second coming. For when he comes, we will either see him as our savior or our destroyer and that is merely determined by where our hearts are at and/or how much oil is left in our lamps. May our lights be burning bright when Jesus comes, showing that we obeyed his great commission as we see him as our savior.

TO SEE A REVIVAL

    Oh to see a revival like what happened in Jesus's day like the day of pentecost. I do not know if it would be too much to want to see a "recipe" for the event known as the day of pentecost. Yet if we read the scriptures of that event and the days leading up to it, we can see dots we can connect that tells a story. We can pick out what looks like ingredients for a recipe. The purpose of following a recipe is to get the same desired results. In the case of desiring to see a revival in the world, what does the scriptures say is the "recipe" for a revival and what is the proof, for the proof is always in the pudding.

    At this point I will make sure that it is known that I am not a scholar and do not see myself as wise, and I am not a pentecostal. I am only a selfish and sinful child that chose to walk with Jesus and had questions. I also believe the words Jesus spoke to his disciple in Matthew 7:7-9.

    As I asked and looked, one day at a time, I saw in scripture basic ingredients for a revival whether it be a personal revival or a mass one. The ingredients seem to simply be belief in Jesus Christ as our Lord and savior, real repentance of our sins/selfishness and then becoming baptized in the name of the Father, Son and Holy Ghost. Afterwards when all ingredients are there and mixed, the Holy Ghost comes to us and quickens our understanding or awakens us. We become spiritually dead no longer. We feel the gap caused by our selfishness bridged by the sacrifice of Jesus through the Holy Ghost, and we begin to feel his presence cleaning house in our heart, mind and eventually body. Many of us have trouble with this because we hear him saying to come as we are and often assume this means we get to stay the way we are and everyone else has to accept it. Jesus makes it clear that a change will and must happen as we walk with him one day at a time. Those that tell others that a change has to happen before baptism, are doing the body of Christ a dis-service and are participating in trying to sell salvation as the Scribes and Pharisees were guilty of. Repentance comes from believing in and on Jesus Christ as our Lord and savior. That repentance is what leads us to want to change and is what the Holy Ghost is waiting for. But in order for the Holy Ghost to enter in to strengthen and inspire us for the process of change, we have to receive baptism. It is only after baptism that we are able to receive the Holy Ghost and start the shaping and molding process.

Matthew 9:16,17

16) "No man putteth a piece of new cloth unto an old garment, for that which is put in to fill it up taketh from the garment, and the rent is made worse.
17) Neither do men put new wine into old bottles: Else the bottles break, and the wine runneth out, and the bottles perish: But they put new wine into new bottles, and both are preserved".

Matthew 6:21-24

21) "For where your treasure is, there will your heart be also.
22) The light of the body is the eye; If therefore thine eye be single, thy whole body shall be full of light.
23) But if thine eye be evil, thy whole body shall be full of darkness. If therefore the light that is in the be darkness, how great is that darkness!
24) No man can serve two masters: for either he will hate the one, and love the other; Or else he will hold to the one, and despise the other. Ye cannot serve God and mammon".

Many of us think that we can be saved and still follow the ways of the world. We continue to listen to music that feeds things like our anger, lusts, envies and our depressions, all because it is what we grew up listening to, or allowed to listen to. We listen to and watch ungodly things, then wonder why we can't beat the things that hold us down. We wonder why we cannot put down chains that Jesus's sacrifice unlocked or why we keep picking them back up. Our walk with Jesus makes us confront these things and we choose to change slowly as we walk with Jesus, or we choose to try to serve two masters. We continue to try to put new spirit into a body holding on to old ways, constantly struggling to make it fit as we have to distort Jesus's lessons to do so. Then we teach our children this watered down faith that teaches us to justify our sins which passes our selfishness from one generation to another. If our walk with Jesus does not make us more careful about what we let our eyes see and our ears to hear, we are still trying to serve two masters; We are still trying to put new spirit in an old self and we will get offended and upset when it is brought to our attention. We immediately try to justify our lifestyle choices just to keep from feeling the regret of passing this same system of serving two masters to our next generations and what it does to them. Jesus does not withhold his teachings just because it makes one's demons nervous so to say.

    The first ingredient for this revival recipe appears to be belief in Jesus Christ as our Lord and savior. This one ingredient seems to be the hardest for many to accept, But it is the most important. Without the belief in his life, death and resurrection, the cake will never rise. Belief in Jesus and his promises is the yeast for this recipe. All of the ingredients are important and if we miss certain ingredients or try to cheat and use inferior ones, the cake just never tastes right. Like a cake, leave out the yeast and it will never rise. Jesus made his part clear in his own words.

John 14:6

6)   Jesus saith unto him, "I am the way, the truth, and the life: No man cometh unto the father, but by me.

    Jesus also makes clear the importance of belief through many of his healing acts. While God can force his will on a mere creation, he chooses not to and so belief becomes like a natural law that is required to return home. We do not receive if we do not believe. I know many do not like this saying because we are eager to throw stones at one another, but we have to ask ourselves, did Jesus say we can be saved by not believing in him and his words? Did he ever say that we can be saved without baptism? No, therefore we have to believe in healing to receive healing. Just like we have to believe in salvation to receive it. Almost like God is simply telling us he does not want those in his kingdom that do not want to be, and if we want to be, we will simply believe and obey. Many try to use the thief on the cross as an excuse to not obey the need for baptisms. Our selfish nature always looks for loopholes out of what we do not want to do. We always try to re-invent ways to do what God has made as simple as possible. It is our selfishness that makes it seem so burdensome. The first problem with using the thief as an example is that it is only a huge assumption that he had never been baptized. It says nowhere that this man was unbaptized. We accuse so many of twisting scriptures yet here is a twist as plain as day. Just like all other plain twists that merely use the excuse that scripture isn't serious. Second is that salvation without baptism is reserved for those that come to the knowledge and belief of Jesus without ever having the chance for baptism, as like being on our deathbed or hanging on a cross. As I mentioned earlier in this book, the thief showed proof of his belief as he defended Jesus from the mockery of the other thief that refused even on the cross, that Jesus was the Christ. The one thief's last actions were works of testifying to the truth of Jesus being who he said he was. Again, making it clear that belief is very important.

Matthew 9:27-30

27) And when Jesus departed thence, two blind men followed him, crying, and saying, thou son of David, have mercy on us.

28) And when he was come unto the house, the blind men came to him: And Jesus saith unto him, "Believe ye that I am able to do this"? They said unto him, yea, Lord.

29) Then touched he their eyes, saying, "According to your faith be it unto you".
30) And their eyes were opened, and Jesus straitly charged them, saying, "see that no man know it".

Luke 7:6-10

6) Then Jesus went with them. And he was now not far from the house, the centurion sent friends to him, saying unto him, Lord, trouble not thyself: For I am not worthy that thou shouldest enter under my roof:
7) Wherefore neither thought I myself worthy to come unto thee: But say in a word, and my servant shall be healed.
8) For I also am a man set under authority, having under me soldiers, and I say unto one, go, and he goeth; And to another, come, and he cometh; And to my servant, do this, and he doeth it.
9) When Jesus heard these things, he marveled at him, and turned him about, and said unto the people that followed him, "I say unto you, I have not found so great a faith, no, not in Israel".
10) And they that were sent, returning to the house, found the servant whole that had been sick.

Luke 8:43-48

43) And a woman having an issue of blood twelve years, which had spent all her living upon physicians, neither could be healed of any,
44) Came behind him, and touched the border of his garment: And immediately her issue of blood stanched.
45) And Jesus said, "Who touched me"? When all denied, Peter and they that were with him said, master, the multitude throng thee and press thee, and sayest thou, who touched me?
46) And Jesus said, "Somebody hath touched me: For I perceive that virtue is gone out of me".
47) And when the woman saw that she was not hid, she came trembling, and falling down before him, she declared unto him before all the people for what cause she had touched him,

and how she was healed immediately.
48) And he said unto her, "Daughter, be of good comfort: Thy faith hath made thee whole; Go in peace".

Jesus never really healed the same way twice that I read of. The only common factor in every healing act was belief not only in Jesus, but that healing came from him. The belief has to be present that Jesus can and will do what he says he can do. So the question always goes back to our belief in Jesus as our Lord and Savior. Note that in each story is an example of being healed and made whole by faith, which is why so many deny works. The mistake of this logic is lucifer blinding us to the fact that each display of faith was only possible by their show of works also, proving that faith and works go hand in hand. We cannot have one without the other. One without the other is only an empty shell. We can gain some relief in knowing that even some like Peter and John the Baptist had trouble with unbelief at times.

Matthew 14:26-31

26) And when his disciple saw him walking on the sea, they were troubled, saying, it is a spirit, and they cried out for fear.
27) But straightway Jesus spoke unto them, saying, "Be of good cheer; It is I; Be not afraid".
28) And Peter answered him and said, Lord, if it be thou, bid me come unto thee on the water.
29) And he said, "come". And Peter was come down out of the ship, he walked on the water, to go to Jesus.
30) But when he saw the wind boisterous, he was afraid; And beginning to sink, he cried, saying, Lord, save me.
31) And immediately Jesus stretched forth his hand, and caught him, and said unto him. "O thou of little faith, wherefore didst thou doubt"?

Luke 7:19,20

19) And John calling unto him two of his disciples sent them to Jesus, saying, art thou he that should come? Or look we for another?

20) When the men were come unto him, they said, John Baptist hath sent us unto the, saying, art thou he that should come? Or look we for another?

Matthew 17:14-20

14) And when they were come to the multitude, there came to him a certain man, kneeling down to him, and saying,
15) Lord, have mercy on my son: For he is lunatic, and sore vexed: For oftimes he falleth into the fire, and oft into the water.
16) And I brought him to thy disciples, and they could not cure him.
17) Then Jesus answered and said, "O faithless and perverse generation, how long shall I be with you? How long shall I suffer You? Bring him hither to me".
18) And Jesus rebuked the devil; And he departed out of him: And the child was cured from that very hour.
19) Then came the disciples to Jesus apart, and said, why could not we cast him out?
20) And Jesus said unto them, "Because of your unbelief: For verily I say unto you, If ye have faith as a grain of mustard seed, Ye shall say unto this mountain, remove hence to yonder place; And it shall remove; And nothing shall be impossible unto you".

Matthew 18:2,3

2) And Jesus called a little child unto him, and set him in the midst of them,
3) And said, "Verily I say unto you, except ye be converted, and become as little children, Ye shall not enter into the kingdom of heaven".

It seems apparent that belief is a huge ingredient and is showed by humbling ourselves like a child, and being pliable and curious to learn and ask questions like a child. To have the desire like a child to ask, seek and knock. This means we believe not only in him, but we believe his words and actions also, like a child. We trust in the promises he gave us as believers like a child. We trust in him full heartedly as a child trusts and believes their loving parents. The sad reality is that lucifer knows these instructions also, so he works hard to make sure that so many do not get to experience these things first from their parents. He keeps us moving faster and faster as we chase things that leave our children starving for the things that we are to show to Jesus. Jesus was serious about his words because he was not only introducing us to the nature of the Father through him; But showing us the steps to salvation, along with teaching how to overcome selfishness with selflessness. Note that when Jesus saved Mary from being stoned, he did not tell her to go and try not to get caught again? He told her to go and sin no more.

    Believing and following Jesus leads us to feel sorry and regretful when we look into that mirror and start seeing how deep the selfishness runs, not only in the world, but within ourselves. Much of selfishness is simply turning a blind eye to all of the deadly sins that our selfishness creates in the world, all to feel accomplished and comfortable and so we do not have to feel responsible. We start to understand why we need a savior. Left alone, the guilt we often feel from this can consume a person like a cancer until we explode on others or self implode, rotting from the inside out. This is the reason for the next ingredient, repentance. The only way to cure the guilt and continue the path of revival is to confront and repent. To repent is to admit of our selfishness. We have to confess to Our Father in Heaven that our selfishness has caused us to do all manner of sins that we cannot pay for. That crumbs from his table are better than anything we can do outside of his presence and this world is the proof. We have to confess that we need the sacrifice of Jesus and his perfect example if we are to ever make it home. This is why Jesus made the sacrifice, to remove the authority from men that were being influenced by lucifer's system of thought, to control forgiveness and salvation by treating it as something to be bought and sold. Jesus did not become our high priest through fulfilling the law of sacrifice, doing away with all sacrifices for good, only to have men that disobey the scriptures and teach others to do the same by saying they are not serious, lie and say we have to go through them for confession and forgiveness. Do some carry such a weight that they need help through the repentance process? Yes; But this does not mean that all must do the same. This certainly does not mean we demean Jesus's sacrifice by telling others we still have to make monetary and/or verbal sacrifices to finish the forgiveness process. This is not biblical and is an insult to our Lord and Savior's sacrifice meant for all those that would merely believe and become baptized. Do we need man still for the baptismal part of the process? Yes. and this is where the system of thought fathered by lucifer still tries to control salvation through men by making it something that seems to have to be bought. It is not given near as freely as it was in Jesus's day. It has been stanched down to a trickle compared to what Jesus had in mind for the great commission.

 Selfishness entangles us in sin so much that no amount of our sacrifices could pay for the debt we owe. No sooner than we think we have shaken off lust and envy, then pride within ourselves blinds us to other sins creeping in. It is a never ending battle that takes more than we have to fight, and can only be fought one day at a time. That is where Jesus comes in. This is why he gave lessons in his parables and lived the example we are to follow one day at a time. All so we can start to see a little of what heaven on earth would look like. It is no wonder that Jesus mentions both moving day by day and his will being done on earth as it is in heaven during the Lord's prayer we are to model as our own.

 With the belief of Jesus and repentance done, now comes baptism. With Jesus being our example to follow, His first example for us was to baptize for the remission of sins. Some see it as being initiated in a club because there seems to be so many different clubs as we have to be baptized into each one. Except, we are baptized into the body of Christ once and it is a show of faith in Jesus that as we go underwater a sinful and selfish person, we come up, a new creation as our past mistakes and selfishness flow downriver out of our lives. It is only after baptism that the Holy Ghost can dwell within us to strengthen us for the shaping and molding process. Many see it as only symbolic, but again, do we believe in Jesus or do we also believe Jesus? Because he not only showed us to do it at the beginning of his ministry, but he still commanded it to be done on his way out.

Now that we have an understanding of how a personal revival can be achieved; Through belief, true repentance and baptism, we can ask how a revival like the day of pentecost can happen. For this we have to keep in mind that while Jesus was with the apostles on earth, the Holy Ghost had not yet been sent. Jesus tells them that he must go so he can send the Holy Ghost as our companion, and that it will be the Holy Ghost that guides us in all truth.

John 16:7-13

7) "Nevertheless I tell you the truth; It is expedient for you that I go away: For If I go not away, the comforter will not come unto you; But if I depart, I will send him unto you.
8) And when he is come, he will reprove the world of sin, and of righteousness, and of judgment:
9) Of sin, because they believe not on me;
10) Of righteousness, because I go to my Father, and ye see me no more;
11) Of judgment, because the prince of this world is judged.
12) I have yet many things to say unto you, but ye cannot bear them now.
13) Howbeit when, the spirit of truth, is come, he will guide you into all truth: For he shall not speak of himself; But whatsoever he shall hear, that shall he speak: And he will shew you things to come".

Once we understand that the spirit could not come until after Jesus left; and that it is the spirit that reveals to us the truth and lessons of Jesus, we can better understand what happened on the day of pentecost. Throughout Jesus's ministry, there was a growth of baptisms going on. John the Baptist appeared to be dunking any head that got within arms reach. It is not certain who all was baptizing, only that it was being done. Numerous people were being baptized, but could not receive the Holy Ghost because Jesus had not ascended yet to send him. Before baptism, it is like the Holy Ghost can only brush up against us, many of us have felt it. After baptism, the Holy Ghost is able to dwell within us as a companion. It is only then that the actual walk with Jesus begins, and it is this walk that starts the shaping and molding process that slowly reveals the selfishness that needs to be chiseled away. We have to choose to remove a chunk of selfishness before we can move on to another. Just like in surgical procedures, if a doctor tries to remove too much too fast, it can be fatal. This is why we show patience with each other, because we are all at different stages of the process we all have to go through. After a time when Jesus ascended, because the Holy Ghost waits until all ingredients are genuine and it brings the most glory to the Father, the believers that were gathered in one accord received the comforter that Jesus spoke of.

Acts 2:1-4

1) And when the day of Pentecost was fully come, they were with one accord in one place.
2) And suddenly there came a sound from heaven as of a rushing mighty wind, and it filled all
the house where they were sitting.
3) And there appeared unto them cloven tongues like as of fire, and it sat upon each of them.
4) And they were filled with the Holy Ghost, and began to speak with other tongues, as the spirit gave them utterance.

This event happened because so many that were baptized previously were gathered together in one place and one accord, or belief. Remember, all ingredients need to be present and genuine. Can we imagine hundreds or even thousands receiving the Holy Ghost all at once? Jesus even tells us what spiritual gifts will follow a real revival. If there are none of the spiritual gifts that he describes following a claimed revival, it is not real. Once we understand the importance of baptism in the revival process, we start understanding why lucifer works so hard to deny baptisms to so many. We see why lucifer would trick people into believing that baptism is not needed despite all of the proof that it is, and why he would trick people into thinking that change has to be complete before receiving baptism. Lucifer knows that this step is required to receive the baptism of the spirit, so he tricks others into treating baptism like something that has to be bought and earned, when it is free to all and the only requirements are belief and repentance. We tend to think that we can judge a person's worthiness yet Jesus tells us that no one comes to him unless the Father sends them. That no person can speak good of Jesus without the influence of the Holy Ghost, and that we are to come to him as we are. The change comes with the walk with Jesus.

John 6:44

44) " No man can come to me, except the Father which hath sent me draw him: And I will raise him up at the last day".

1 Corinthians 12:3

3) Wherefore I give you to understand, that no man speaking by the spirit of God calleth Jesus accursed: And that not man can say that Jesus is the Lord, but by the Holy Ghost.

So yes, there is a recipe to follow that lucifer tricks mankind into deviating from and complicating. Mankind's habit is to change and complicate things. It is how many of us make ourselves feel important, needed and/or accomplished. It is also how the wicked gain power and control over others. Even the religious leaders of Jesus's day who sat in Moses's seat were guilty of lucifer's tricks of trying to control forgiveness and salvation. If we want to see a personal revival in our own lives, we have to follow the recipe, believe in Jesus's words and actions. That belief convicts us to repent and repentance leads us to baptism. After baptism, not always right away, The Holy Ghost comes to us as our guide and comforter on our walk with Jesus. The Holy Ghost does not always come right away because many of us do not always get baptized for the right reasons. Only the Holy Ghost knows when everything is genuine and will bring the most glory to God the Father. Only he knows how bright our light will shine and for how long. Some lights burn steady over a lifetime while some burn brilliantly but for a short time. It is for the Holy Ghost to determine when to appear in a person's life, it is only ours to baptize and teach of Jesus.

    If we want to see mass revivals, we have to do what the great commission says and go out into all the world baptizing all in the name of the Father, Son and Holy Ghost. We should be dunking every head that the Father draws close enough to be dunked, then let the Holy Ghost take over as we continue teaching about all that Jesus has said and done. We should not be acting like only one member of the body of Christ has the authority to baptize. When we are baptized, we are baptized into the whole body of Christ, not just a single body part. Yet we see lucifer's influence as one body part of Christ or denomination denies the authority of another. Not one place in the bible says we have to pay a single tithe to receive baptism or forgiveness. I am not saying that tithing is not a thing, I am saying that requiring any form of payment in order to receive baptism is not biblical at all, and falls under the category of trying to sell salvation, knowing that baptism is a part of the process of salvation. It actually falls right in with lucifer's agenda to keep as many as possible from obtaining baptism which puts a roadblock on our road to salvation. Pastors of all denominations could be baptizing hundreds and thousands but they fight over whether one or the other has the authority to baptize, or simply afraid that the one they baptized won't end up in their house of prayer paying their tithes. This division only scatters those ready for harvest as we see the division and become confused on where to even go. The Apostle Paul addresses this issue as the people of his day fresh with the influence of Jesus, and the apostles fight amongst themselves just like today's denominations.

1 Corinthians 1:10-15

10) Now I beseech you, brethren, by the name of our Lord Jesus Christ, that ye all speak the same thing, and that there be no divisions among you; But that ye be perfectly joined together in the same mind and in the same judgment.
11) For it hath been declared unto me of you, my brethren, by them which are of the house of chloe, that there are contentions among you.
12) Now this I say, that every one of you saith, I am of Paul; and I of Apollos; and I of Cephas; and I of Christ.
13) Is Christ divided? Was Paul crucified for you? Or were ye baptized in the name of Paul?
14) I thank God that I baptized none of you, but Crispus and Gaius;
15) Lest any should say that I had baptized in mine own name.

It is not that the early houses of prayer were actually baptizing people in their own name, just as houses of prayer today do not do the same. What they are doing the same today as they did then that Paul is chastising them for, is dividing the houses of prayer based on who started that particular house of prayer. A house that Peter started was acting mightier than a house another apostle started. It was the start of the very divisions we see today with the different denominations. They are divided and not of one accord, throwing stones at each other arguing over who the greatest is just like the apostles when Jesus caught them arguing over the same topic. They started caring more about the individual houses of prayer than the gifts of the spirit, until the individual gifts became tools for division also, until each gift given to profit all was denied by each other. I do not feel that the letters to the church of old would read much differently if written for today's denominations. I believe they would include a chastisement for building a gate around baptismal water only to charge admission, then covet the spiritual gifts given to profit the whole body of Christ in the works to fulfill the great commission. Because of the damning up of the flow of baptisms, the flow of mass and personal revivals are slowed to a trickle. With the size of the modern population, and if we were all proving our belief in Jesus by fulfilling the great commission so that the spirit can do his part, the spider webbing of baptisms should be making its own spider webbing of revivals both personal and mass.

    I pray that we all will humble ourselves and quit trying to be more than we are. This very line of logic is the cause of lucifer's fall from grace. I pray that we will break the cycle of the Scribes and Pharisees of complicating what Jesus simplified in order to control and profit off of forgiveness and salvation. I pray we will stop withholding baptisms like it is ours to give away, instead of something we were commissioned to go out and do. I pray that we would stop treating forgiveness as something that doesn't only come from Jesus Christ our Lord and savior. Finally, I pray we would see revivals around the world as we freely baptize masses, and learn that our baptismal fonts are way too small for what Jesus had in mind, And the poetry in motion that should be the Holy Ghost awakening the spiritually dead on mass scales. In the end, the question will be whether we were a part of the spreading of revival, or a part of staunching the flow?

POETRY IN MOTION

While this book is titled poetry in motion, I named this chapter the same to share a few road experiences that show examples of the Holy Ghost working hard to work all things for good. It is our selfish desires that get in the way of the Holy Ghost and his work. It is our selfish desires that cause every problem we blame God for. When we slow down and put our selfishness aside, we come closer to working for the profit of all and aligning with the Father's will. We then see the poetry in motion that is the Holy Ghost, working in each life like an app that most do not know is there, trying to work all things to good.

    I sometimes think of the spirits job like a roomba. He is constantly working hard to clean up the messes that humanity's selfishness creates in order to clean as much as possible before the Father gets home. Being patient and selfless helps the roomba clean. Being selfish and hasty creates more messes to clean up and makes it harder for it to maneuver. Do not get me wrong, I still fight my own selfishness on a day to day basis just like everyone else. The Holy Ghost taught me that it becomes easier when we take things one day at a time. It took me almost 2 years of trying to really start understanding. A lot of our selfishness creates impatience and impatience works against the Holy Ghost and his work. It becomes harder for the Holy Ghost to get the right people to the right place, at the right time, when we let our selfishness let us become hasty. Anger usually becomes a big factor with impatience. I have witnessed a lot of this as my wife and I drove across the United States. As a transport driver that delivers campers all over America, I saw much room for improvement in my own life with patience as I learned to slow down and look. I found that it is easy to get lost in the attempt to not get angry at others, especially bad drivers. Mainly because it is usually too hard so we end up giving up on the attempt. As I applied the philosophy of one day at a time, I began to realize that the battle with anger is not only about not getting mad. But also about how long we stay angry when we do. I found over time that when I did get mad at something, the time I stayed mad got shorter and shorter. We get to a point where we get angry less often simply because we know we will not stay mad for long, so it becomes less worth getting angry to begin with. This is how I no longer get mad at traffic jams or other delays in life. In this, we make the Holy Ghost's job easier by learning to go with the flow, or with the grain.

    This first story took place in Georgia as my wife and I were on our way to deliver two campers to Florida. We each drive and live in our ram trucks. I carry the piece that the Holy Ghost commissioned me to do in the back of my truck. It is mounted and designed so that I can raise it if I felt led to. As we were driving, my truck went into limp mode and was stuck in 4th gear. Luckily it was right at an exit that had two truck stops. We parked both trucks and campers and I pulled out my scan tool. The scan narrowed it down to my transmission module. Learning to go one day at a time means also learning to go moment by moment. We left my truck and trailer and proceeded to Florida to deliver my wife's trailer. We then drove back to pick up my trailer and go back to Florida to deliver it. During the shuttle trips I was talking to a friend and got all of the info I needed. We had stopped at different places along the way to get the fluid, parts and tools for the job. I watch videos on the job and pray until I feel I can do the job. I parked my truck toward the back of the parking lot with my Jesus piece facing the semi pumps, facing away from the road. Honestly, I was kinda hiding. I was already nervous about the job and I didn't really want to be distracted by anyone.

    As I was working, A truck pulled up and two guys got out and are already tearing up as they look at the mirror on this piece. We begin to talk and I tell them the story about the piece and the lessons it represents. The gentleman that was in the passenger seat explained to me that he was a minister and is in a rough patch. Seeing the piece with the mirror reminded him of why he had gotten into ministry to begin with. The gentleman driving said he was not even sure why he took this exit because they did not need fuel or a restroom. He felt drawn to this truck stop and did not see my truck until he pulled into the lot. He only saw the cross laid down from the front because I was kinda hiding. He got the urge to see it even though the minister said they see people with crosses all of the time. The driver said no, this is different. When they got close enough to see it, they didn't even park straight. We talked for about thirty minutes about Jesus in a truck stop parking lot in tears. "Where two or three are gathered together in my name, there I am with them also". They both expressed how much they needed to see that, even though I was hiding, and they went on their way. I finished the job praising God and went to bed that night ready to leave the next day.

    Or so I thought. I went to leave the next morning and the truck would not shift out of first gear. Since I got the new module at a parts store, my friend said that about five out of seven of those are usually faulty. So I bought a new one from the dealership. While changing the part again, I found that I had lost a rubber during the first job and this is why the truck would not shift gears, not because of a faulty module. Even during this I learned to not get mad, I started looking for the experience. We ended up having to wait three days in Georgia for a five dollar rubber I lost. My wife didn't mind because she got a motel room for about four nights all together.

    Since I got the message that I can't hide, I went ahead and stood the piece up for the three days we were waiting. One day I decided to change my oil and diesel filters. While I was working, an elderly lady approached and asked if she could get a picture. I told her that she was more than welcome to. We talked about Jesus and she shared about growing up in America as a believer of color. She told me, "You know what I like about this piece"? I said what is that Miss Pearl, Pearl was her name. She said, "It's color". I told Miss Pearl that we have to be careful. Even those that portray Jesus as white. Not a single person knows what shade of skin Jesus had and that is a good thing. Jesus was not white or black, he was a Hebrew. It is guaranteed that anyone that gets lost in the color game will be blinded and miss the lessons of Jesus. Because Jesus makes it clear that hate and contention have no part in him, and racism is the breeder of both. We talked more about her childhood and her concerns for her culture. She teared up as I explained the lessons of this piece for all cultures as a body. I felt the spirit tell me that she needed a hug but I'm not one to hug a stranger, especially in a truck stop parking lot. So I asked her if I could give her a hug. She did not speak, only took a step forward. So I took a step and gave her a hug. After a moment, I felt her sobbing on my shoulder. We said goodbye and she left saying that God was going to bless me. I still think of this sweet woman from time to time.

    The part came in and I carefully put everything back together. Everything worked good and we went back to Indiana for our next loads. Even though these were only people that needed encouragement and not a miracle event, It does not make less the need for people to fill these rolls as the Holy Ghost guides. Learning to work with the Holy Ghost is way less stressful than working against, always being angry
trying to force our way, missing the poetry in motion along the way. It is not a one sided exchange that only builds our ego. I learned things myself about trust and not hiding what is meant to encourage others. I learned from both encounters making it a give and take or push and pull experience. None of which would have occurred if I had panicked or became angry and impatient.

    This next experience happened in Buttonwillow, Ca. I had delivered my trailer in Bakersfield, Ca and we had to stop in Buttonwillow because of the high winds. We parked my wife's truck and trailer at the truck stop. I parked my truck next to hers where I could stand the Jesus piece up. The wind was going to be high the next day as well so I got my wife a motel room across the road. I slept in the truck like we do since I had the piece stood up and it stays busy on this little street in Buttonwillow.

    The next day I sat in my folding chair with my sound system playing my playlist. The wind was still too high for us to leave with the camper. As it was getting close to lunch, I walked to the truck stop to get my wife some tacos. Before I walked to the restaurant, I noticed a pickup at the pumps pulling an old camper. He was there for about 20 minutes and was still there when I came out with the tacos. As I walked by his passenger side he hollered at me, just in a way to get my attention. He called me over and asked me if I was with the ministry by the road. I reluctantly told him I was, mainly because I still am not used to it being called a ministry. He asked me what church I was affiliated with and I told him quickly that I am a member of Christ's church. He then asked me where this church meets or is located. Again, I quickly tell him wherever two or three gather in his name. The gentleman asks if he can come over to talk to me. He had been in that spot arguing with the Holy Ghost who told him to talk to me. His mind was made up when I walked by for tacos.

    He pulled his truck and camper over where my truck was. He stayed in his truck and had a look like he was trying to figure out how to say what he wanted to say. I could see tears forming in his eyes as he looked at the piece and looked away. He was fidgeting with a pocket knife then put it down after he realized it I guess. After a few moments of silence I ask him what he had going on. At this point I could smell the alcohol and saw the signs because I had been there and done that. He looks at me with tears saying, " I know what I am supposed to do". He holds up a well worn and marked bible and explains to me that he is a minister who is having a hard time, and has been traveling trying to get his head straight. He was on his way home and ran out of fuel and money two hundred miles from home.

    I told him the story of the piece and my Apostle Paul experience with alcohol. He understood then that I knew where he was at. We talked about Jesus and how the Apostle Paul went through the same problem of doing what we are not supposed to yet wanting to do good but keep picking bad. We topped him off so he could make it home. As I was topping him off, because I always like to make sure they were really on empty, which he was, he started reading my mission statement for this piece and his whole demeanor changed. He looked clear eyed and with a look of a professor grading an essay. He said that he did not know me well enough to know if I have other gifts, but he was certain I had the gift of teaching. I do not know about that because I am only a selfish fool with only a high school education.

He called his wife to let her know that he would be home that day and told her about me helping him out. He put her on speaker and they each said a prayer for the help and for the ministry. He was definitely reminded of why he got into the ministry to begin with and left with a light in his eyes. I was left to think about the poetry in motion as the spirit tries to lead the right people, to the right place, at the right time, all for the profit of all. As we become able to see this poetry in motion, we start understanding how our selfishness and impatience leaves a lot of holes meant to be filled by the right people. Instead, our eagerness to be in a hurry and succeed at any cost, makes us miss many opportunities to do good for others.

This last example took place in a small town between Arroyo Grande, Ca and Barstow, Ca. My wife and I had both delivered our trailers after shuttling them with my wife's truck from Barstow because my fan clutch went out coming over the mountains. We were on our way back to Barstow from Arroyo Grande. The roads in between are farm roads and there are not many stations. The mountain passes can stick you behind slow semis. You can either settle in for the slow haul, or get mad and hotrod around them. Three years into trying to live day by day, along with having six hundred thousand on my wife's truck, so I just settled in. My wife and I both had to pee after a couple of slow semis. She shuns the first two small stations we passed because she wasn't sure about the cleanliness. We finally see a better station so I pull in knowing my wife needs to go. We go inside and head toward the restrooms. As I walk by the register, I notice a kid, maybe in his twentys. He is standing in line holding a food item and an energy drink. We get to the restrooms and both doors are locked. My wife says that we may need a key because nobody answered when she knocked. As I go back to the register to ask about a key, I see the energy drink and food item on the floor. I get in line looking at the kid standing up and I am wondering why he dropped his stuff. I saw the kid lean a bit, I assumed because of the weight of his backpack. I hear the clerk ask him what he is doing. He leans over a bit more as his arms pull up to his chest with his fingers contorted. I looked around and everyone was frozen in place. Nobody moved to catch what I was seeing in slow motion I guess.

    As the backpack pulled him back, all I could see in my mind's eye was his backpack making his head slingshot toward the concrete as his pack would make contact first since he was planking. I looked around again to see everyone frozen in place, so I stepped around him and supported him to keep him from planking backwards. I propped him up as I looked around telling people that I do not know what to do. He was heavier than me so I finally had to let him sit and lay back. He started to shake and someone finally told me to roll him over and watch his head. As he shook, I told Jesus that if he was going to help me now would be the time. I felt the Holy Ghost tell me to shush him. I almost did not listen. I could hear the clerk on the phone with 911 and I saw all of the people staring, not doing anything. I finally quit looking and pushed down any embarrassment, because that is what it boiled down to. I looked at this stranger shaking in my arms and started shushing him like a baby. After a couple of shushes I even started petting his head. For just a moment, this kid was not a stranger. He was a brother that needed help. After only fifteen or twenty seconds, he came out of it and got up trying to walk it off. I'm sure it was odd for him. Last he knew he was standing in line. Next he wakes up on the floor with a gnome looking guy shushing him and petting his head.

My wife and I left after the fire department showed up. We left with the sense of awe in the poetry in motion of the events. From my fan clutch going out making us have to shuttle trailers to the simplest thing like getting stuck behind a slow semi, If we slow down to look, we can see the evidence of the Holy Ghost trying to once again, work all things for the good of all. These are only a few of the many experiences we have had traveling over the years, trying to show everyone who we need to put our eyes back on in order to heal this society. These are only a few that show the importance of living day by day and sometimes, moment by moment. The importance of not letting this world make us impatient and always in a hurry. This will always lead us to miss that still small voice that is the Holy Ghost and his poetry in motion. This is something that I still find myself lacking even after three years into trying to live these lessons of Jesus. I pray that we all will strive to endure to the end, trying to be better each day. I pray that as we learn to enter into the rest of the seventh day sabbath, we will be reminded of the love, life and time that he blesses us with each day; and that it pleases him when we use these blessings of love, life and time for the profit of all. I pray that we will see that the rejuvenation we receive on the seventh day of rest helps us to take things one day at a time, and allows us to slow down to hear that still small voice that is the Holy Ghost working in all things. Finally, may the Father shelter us, Jesus forgive and heal us and the Holy Ghost guide, direct and comfort us on our way home, Amen.

AUTHOR'S NOTE

    I was led to write this note because it is not only the administrations or denominations that throw stones at each other scattering the flock. Many operations or ministries throw stones at each other also, thinking that one ministry is better than another. We often get so rooted in what we alone like or agree with, we forget how diverse the Holy Ghost has to be to draw so many different people to Jesus. We know that there is only one way to God the Father, but there are multiple ways to Jesus. Or did every person that has ever come to Jesus come to him through the same experience? Did each apostle come to Jesus the same way? While we all have to go through the same process to come the same understanding, it is that understanding that the Holy Ghost is waiting for. Not everyone has to be slapped from their horse to reach this understanding. Our level of stubborness sometimes determines how rough the Holy Ghost has to get with us. I look at it through my carving experience. We can put a finish coat on a completed carving, then put it outside to face the conditions of weather. The longer it sits in bad conditions, the deeper the damage goes. If a refinish job is not done often enough; because there will always be damage when sitting in bad conditions too long and often; the rougher sandpaper we have to use in order to get deep enough to remove all of the bad. Only then can we sand with finer and finer paper until it is smooth enough to reapply the new finish coat. Our stubbornness with the flow of the Holy Ghost and God's plan of salvation is the same.

    I bring this up because of those that might throw stones at my playlist, because it contains Christian rap. I have heard many say that if it does not come out of a hymn book then it is not Christian. Where is this written in scripture? I seem to remember the scriptures saying that the Holy Ghost will turn all bad things for good. Are we once again twisting scripture merely over something we may not like ourselves? Are we going to put limits on what the Holy Ghost may use? Too many are quick to judge because of how lucifer has used rap to promote wickedness, yet forget that the Holy Ghost can use rap to reach the same people that will only listen to rap. Again, lucifer tricks those eager to judge to push away those, "not with us", before evaluating the fruits first. Many hear the music and never listen to the words and message, judging a book by its cover. Is it for everybody, no. It is for those that need to hear things of God but will only listen to rap due to their upbringing and limited influences. I do not see the judgemental people that would wrongly judge this music going into the ghettos preaching Jesus.

    I pray that we would not be so quick to judge without looking for the fruits first. I pray that we would understand that there are diversities of ministries and that includes music meant to reach, inspire and encourage a culture or group of people that would only listen to rap. Many artists that grew up in dark places found Jesus, and the Holy Ghost put in their hearts to reach backinto that darkness with a different message than what lucifer is pushing. Again, many are too eager to throw stones to see it. Just like with this piece I was commissioned by the Holy Ghost to make, if one is offended by the color of the piece, it means that one has an inner problem that needs to be addressed to our Father in Heaven. If one is repulsed by music without ever listening to the message, again there is an inner problem that needs to be taken to the Lord in prayer.

    Finally, I pray we all will realize how universal the lessons are of there being many parts to a body, and how these parts are being used by the Holy Ghost to reach those from a wide variety of walks of life. So if it isn't for you, that's ok. But if it is encouraging others to turn from wickedness and turn to Jesus, I pray we would put up our bag of stones before upsetting the Holy Ghost for denying what he chooses to use. In the end, I pray we could see the poetry in motion as the Holy Ghost uses many things to turn what was meant for evil, to good that reaches the hearts of those that might only hear of Jesus through music first. May we never be the one that denies or forbids what might be the source of them hearing about Jesus, and the desire that this introduction may spark to ask and learn more.

ABOUT THE AUTHOR

    First off, this book is not about me, it is about our Lord and Savior Jesus Christ and how he is real and still works in our lives today. It is a testimony to the fact that Jesus is who he says he is and that his words are true and can be believed. This book is about the Holy Ghost that helps Jesus complete the plan of salvation, giving all praise and glory to God the Father. About the poetry in motion that is the Holy Ghost working all things for the will of the Father through Jesus Christ. This story goes on in the lives of so many that do not realize it because of how fast we live our lives. Each of us has a story of poetry in motion that is capable of lifting others and encouraging each other on our journey of change with Jesus.

    My part in this is nothing more than what any body part is in a whole body. A tool used for a purpose. The Lord used my experience and my occupations to make a piece that points out important lessons needed for a people that are being engulfed in their own selfishness. A piece that is a visual aid only, to help illustrate the lessons that point how to weather the storms that our selfishness creates not only in our personal lives, but in governments, religion and even cultures, as well as the consequences to the body when parts get their magnets backwards. The lesson is that Jesus's system of thought is what was started and lived by in the Garden of Eden. From the time that lucifer's selfishness infected humanity, we started a downward spiral from God's ways and we see the shortening of health and lifespan as it happens. The only true reset is a return to Jesus's system of thought and like it took a long time for our selfishness to get this bad, it takes time to get back and keeping our eyes on Jesus and what he did for us on the cross, is the only way to be lead back out of the darkness.

I am only a nobody that reached too far and was too stubborn. I am a low educated fool that only had experiences from multiple talents to work with. I am no different than anyone else. We all struggle daily against some form of selfishness, the difference is who we get our strength from. It took me falling off of my high horse to hear that still small voice that is the Holy Ghost trying to prepare us for when the bridegroom returns. I am nothing more than a selfish man that found forgiveness and was set on a path and a mission to share about Jesus and the lessons he wants us all to remember in these days and times. Some might say that even in this I am being selfish, because God says that if we see a brother walking towards a cliff and do not warn him, his blood is partly on us; But if we warn our brother and he does not listen, his blood is on his own hands fully, Ezekiel 3:18-21. I pray that we will take the time to learn Jesus's words and take them seriously, so we may learn the lessons that will help us overcome the selfishness that is tearing this world apart. I pray we understand that it is all about Jesus carrying out the will of the Father through the Holy Ghost, and it is our selfishness that is the problem.

www.ingramcontent.com/pod-product-compliance
Lightning Source LLC
Chambersburg PA
CBHW042115100526
44587CB00025B/4057

www.ingramcontent.com/pod-product-compliance
Lightning Source LLC
Chambersburg PA
CBHW042115100526
44587CB00025B/4057